DISNEY THEATRICAL PRODUCTION
under the direction of
Peter Schneider and Thomas Schumacher
presents

AIDA

Music by
ELTON JOHN

Lyrics by
TIM RICE

Book by
LINDA WOOLVERTON
and
ROBERT FALLS & DAVID HENRY HWANG

SUGGESTED BY THE OPERA

Original Cast

HEATHER HEADLEY   ADAM PASCAL   SHERIE RENÉ SCOTT
JOHN HICKOK   DAMIAN PERKINS
TYREES ALLEN   DANIEL ORESKES

ROBERT M. ARMITAGE   TROY ALLAN BURGESS   FRANNE CALMA
CHRIS PAYNE DUPRÉ   THURSDAY FARRAR   KELLI FOURNIER   BOB GAYNOR
KISHA HOWARD   TIM HUNTER   YOUN KIM   KYRA LITTLE   KENYA UNIQUE MASSEY
CORINNE McFADDEN   PHINEAS NEWBORN III   JODY RIPPLINGER   RAYMOND RODRIGUEZ
ERIC SCIOTTO   TIMOTHY EDWARD SMITH   ENDALYN TAYLOR-SHELLMAN
SAMUEL N. THIAM   JERALD VINCENT   SCHELE WILLIAMS   NATALIA ZISA

Scenic & Costume Design
BOB CROWLEY

Lighting Design
NATASHA KATZ

Sound Design
STEVE C. KENNEDY

Hair Design
DAVID BRIAN BROWN

Makeup Design
NAOMI DONNE

Music Arrangements
GUY BABYLON
PAUL BOGAEV

Orchestrations
STEVE MARGOSHES
GUY BABYLON
PAUL BOGAEV

Dance Arrangements
BOB GUSTAFSON
JIM ABBOTT
GARY SELIGSON

Music Coordinator
MICHAEL KELLER

Technical Supervision
THEATRESMITH, INC.

Fight Director
RICK SORDELET

Casting
BERNARD TELSEY CASTING

Development Casting
JAY BINDER

Associate Producer
MARSHALL B. PURDY

Press Representative
BONEAU/BRYAN-BROWN

Production Stage Manager
CLIFFORD SCHWARTZ

Music Produced and Musical Direction by
PAUL BOGAEV

Choreography by
WAYNE CILENTO

Directed by
ROBERT FALLS

Originally developed at the Alliance Theatre Company in Atlanta, Georgia

ISBN 0-634-04802-3

Wonderland Music Company, Inc.

DISTRIBUTED BY

7777 W. BLUEMOUND RD. P.O. BOX 13819 MILWAUKEE, WI 53213

© Disney

In Australia Contact:

Hal Leonard Australia Pty. Ltd.
22 Taunton Drive P.O. Box 5130
Cheltenham East, 319 2 Victoria, Australia
Email: ausadmin@halleonard.com

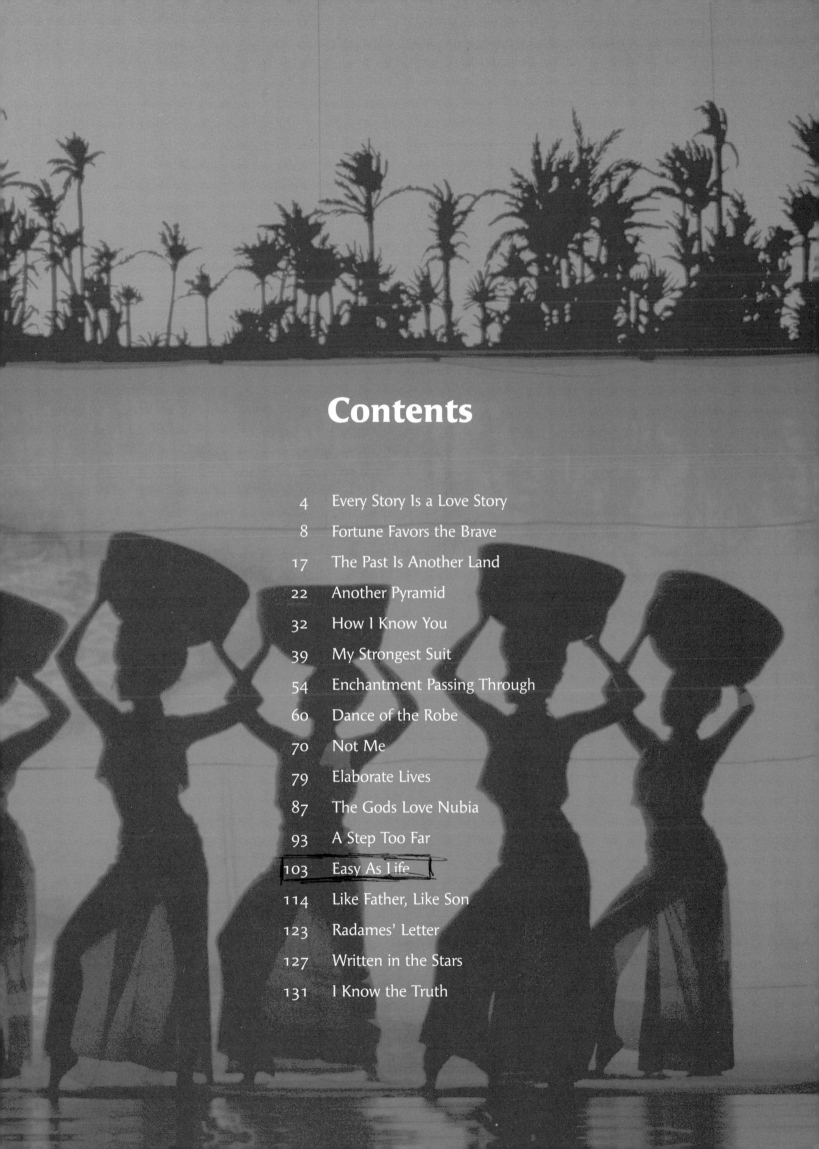

Contents

EVERY STORY IS A LOVE STORY

Music by ELTON JOHN
Lyrics by TIM RICE

In two

Gentle two

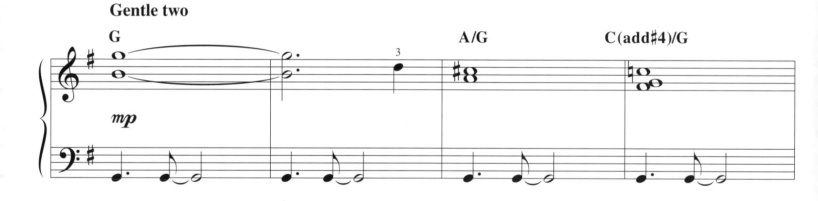

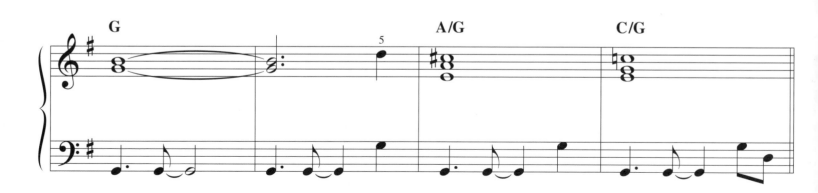

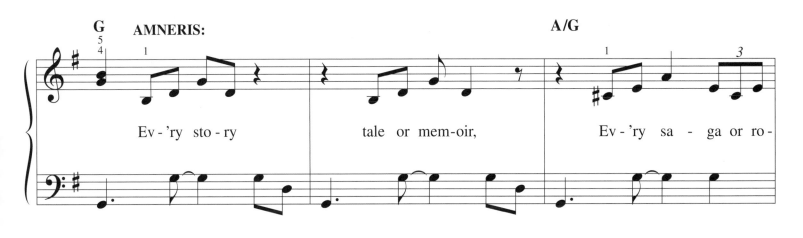

AMNERIS:

Ev - 'ry sto - ry   tale or mem-oir,   Ev - 'ry sa - ga or ro-

mance,   Wheth - er true   or   fab - ri - cat - ed,

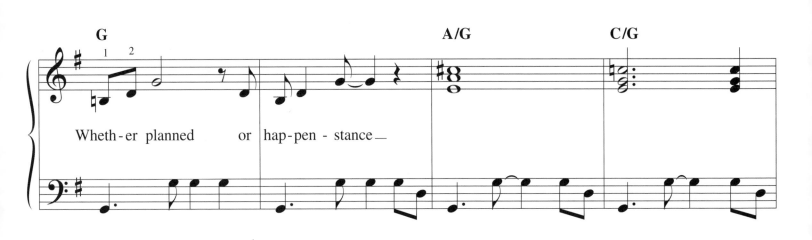

Wheth - er planned   or hap-pen - stance—

Wheth - er sweep-ing   through the ag - es,   cast-ing cen - tu - ries a-

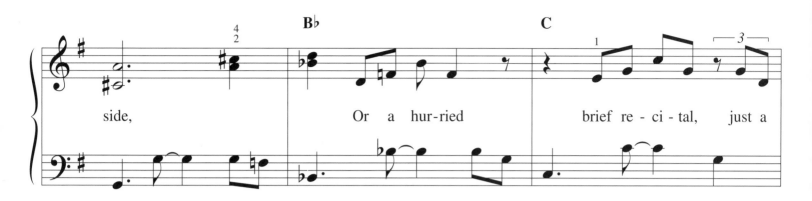

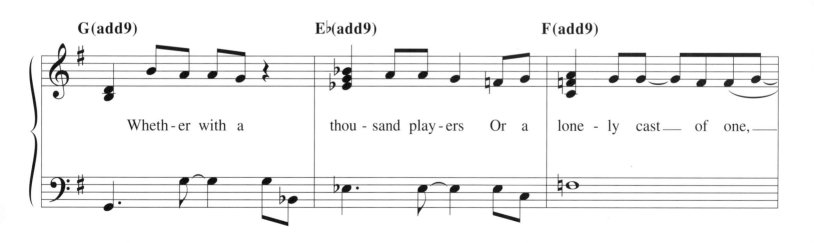

ime

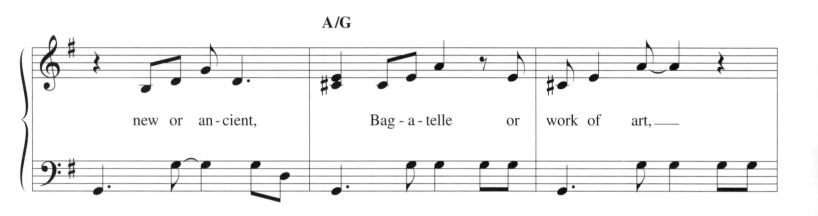

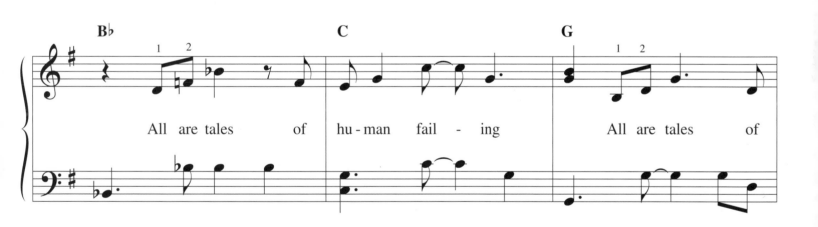

FORTUNE FAVORS THE BRAVE

Music by ELTON JOHN
Lyrics by TIM RICE

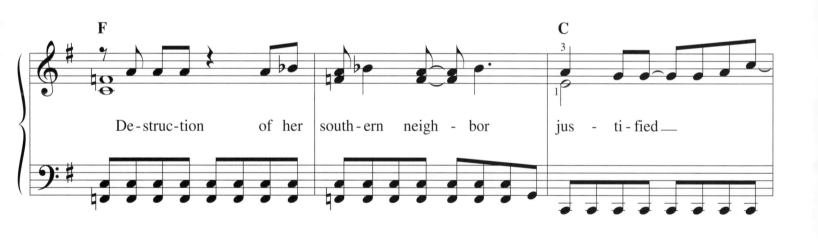

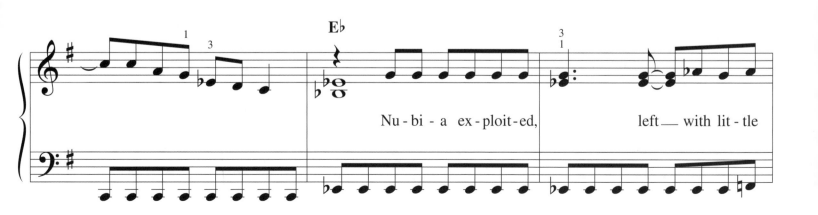

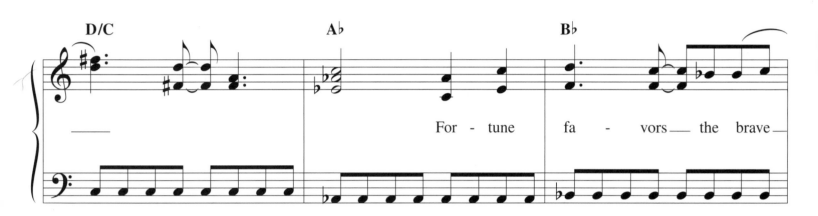

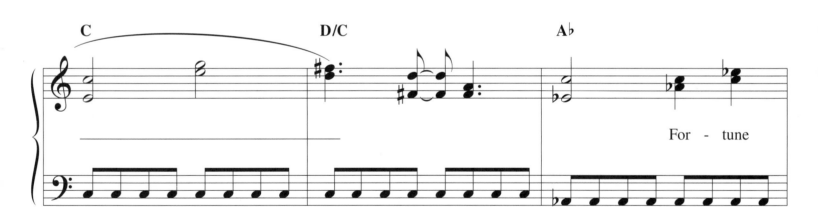

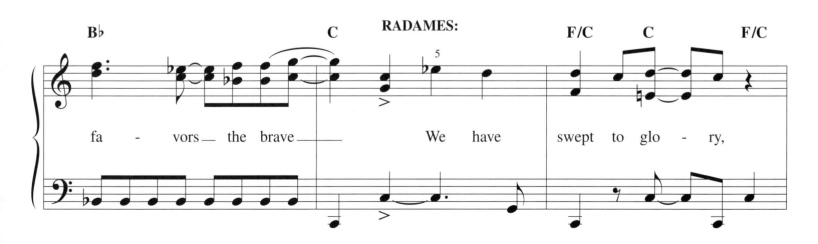

E - gypt's mas - ter - y ____ ex - pands ____ From the Nile's ____ north -

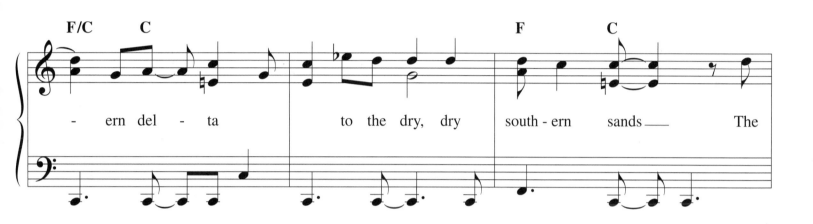

- ern del - ta   to the dry, dry   south - ern sands ____ The

more   we find, ____   the   more we see, ____   the   more ____ we come ____ to learn

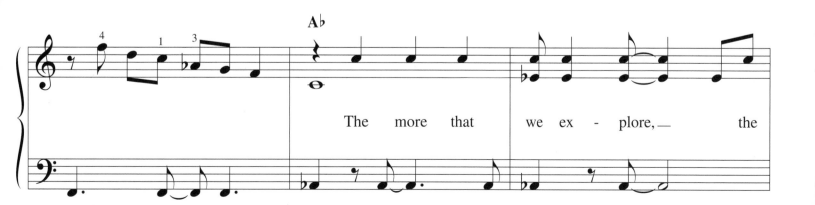

The   more that   we ex - plore, ____   the

more — we shall re - turn — Oh

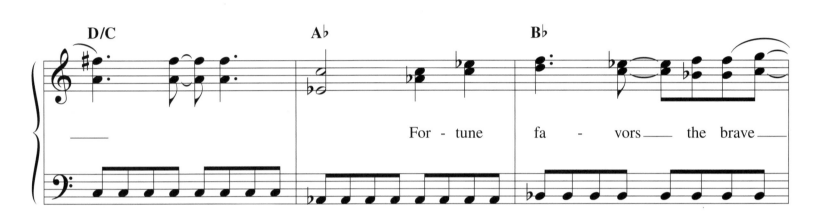

— For - tune fa - vors — the brave —

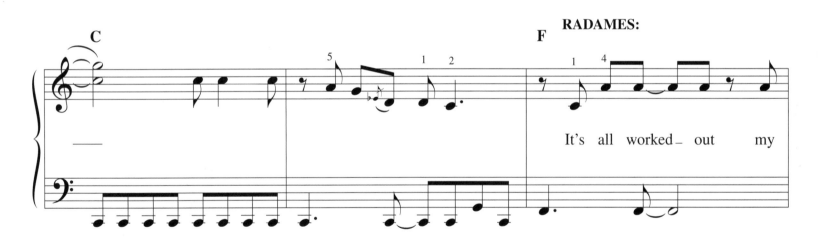

— It's all worked — out my

road is clear — The lines of — lat - i - tude — ex - tend —

13

Way be-yond my wild - est dreams ___ To - ward some great tri - umph-

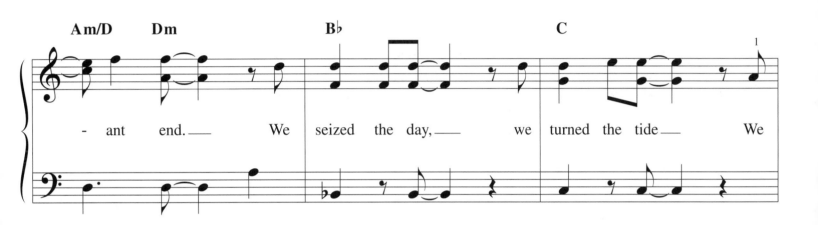

- ant end. ___ We seized the day, ___ we turned the tide ___ We

touched the stars, ___ we mocked the grave ___ We moved in-to ___ un - chart-

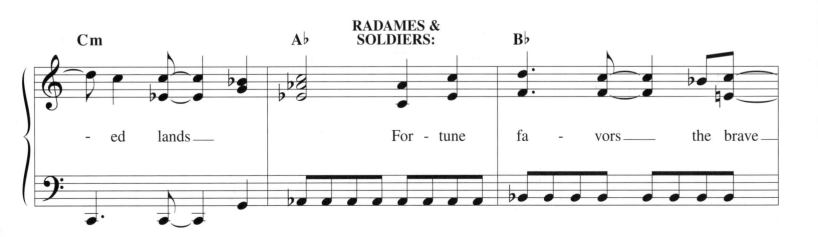

RADAMES & SOLDIERS:

- ed lands ___ For - tune fa - vors ___ the brave

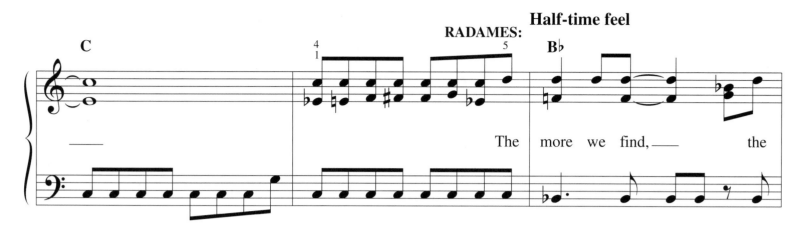

Half-time feel

RADAMES:

The more we find,___ the

more we see,___ the more__ we come__ to learn

The more that we ex - plore,___ the more__ we shall re - turn

___ Noth - ing is an ac - ci - dent___

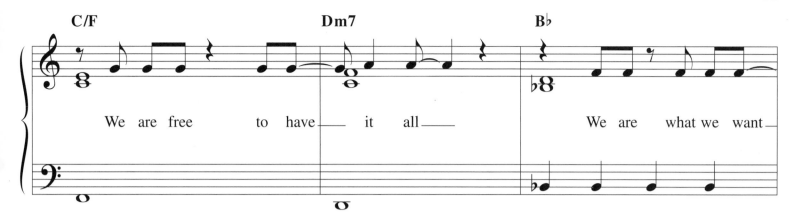

We are free to have it all ___ We are what we want

___ to be It's in our-selves to rise ___ or fall ___

This is eas-y to ___ be-lieve ___ When dis-tant plac-es call

___ to me ___ It's hard-er from ___ the pal-ace yard ___

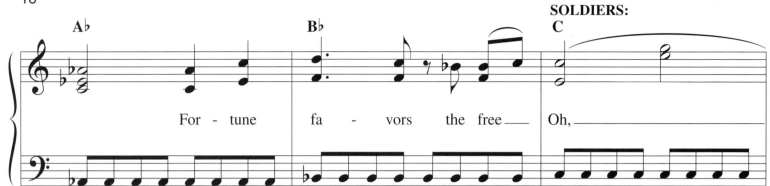

For - tune fa - vors the free ___ Oh, ___

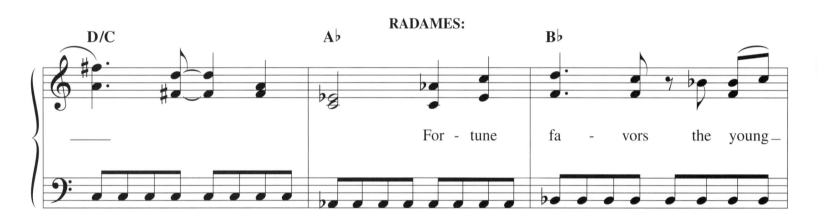

For - tune fa - vors the young ___

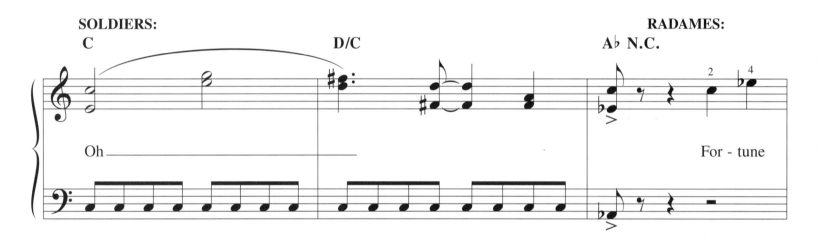

Oh ___ For - tune

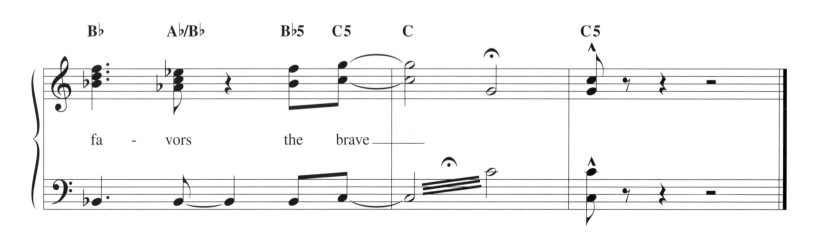

fa - vors the brave ___

THE PAST IS ANOTHER LAND

Music by ELTON JOHN
Lyrics by TIM RICE

The

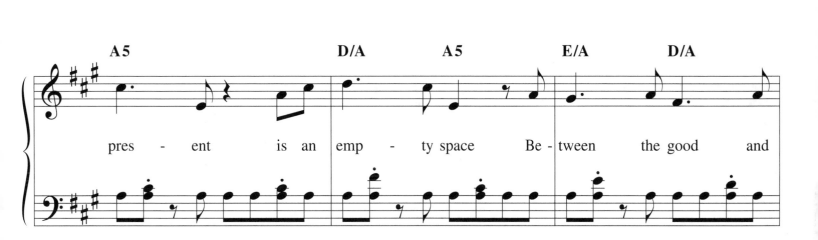

pres - ent is an emp - ty space Be - tween the good and

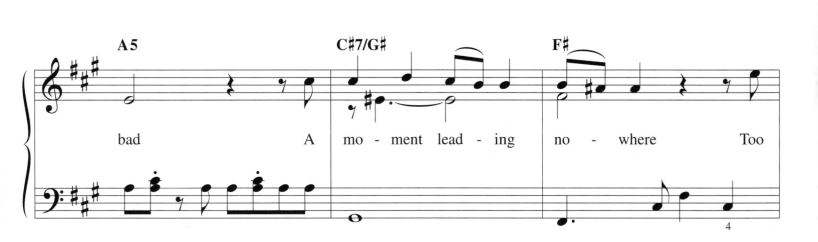

bad A mo - ment lead - ing no - where Too

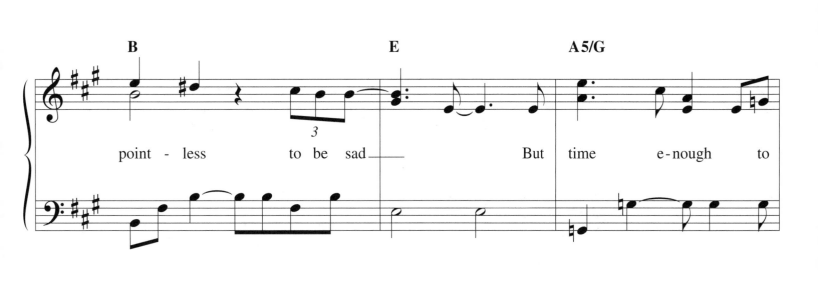

point - less to be sad But time e-nough to

20

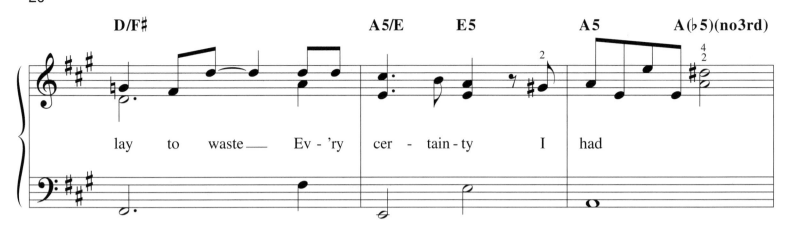

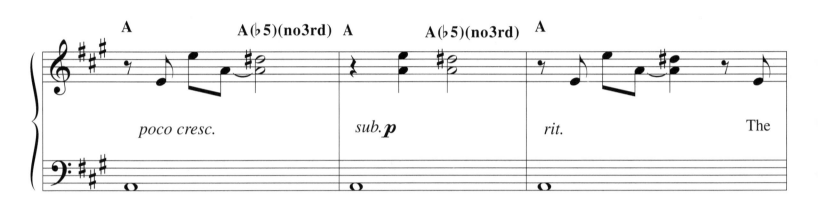

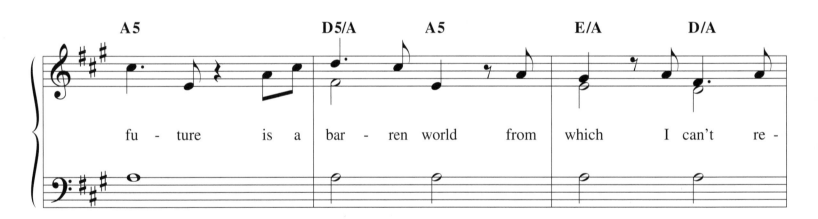

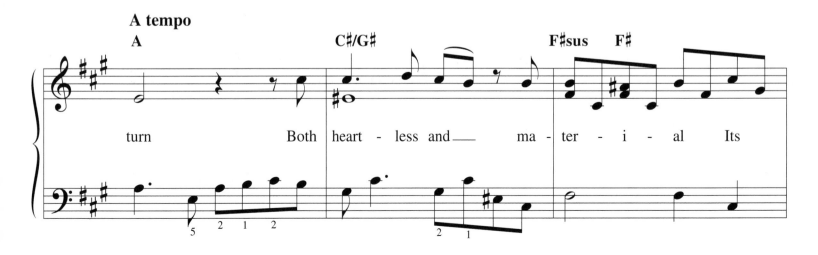

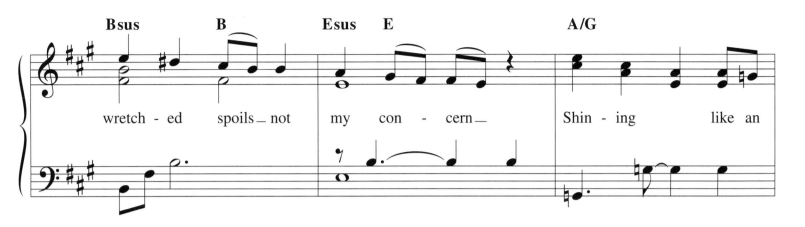

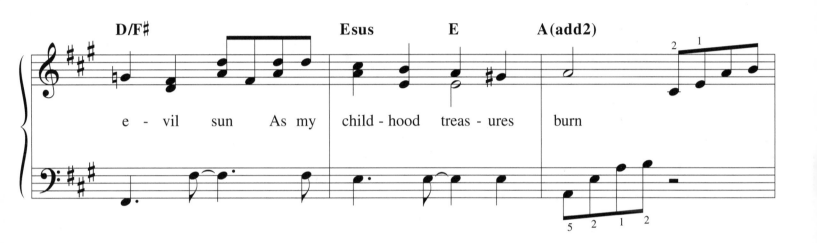

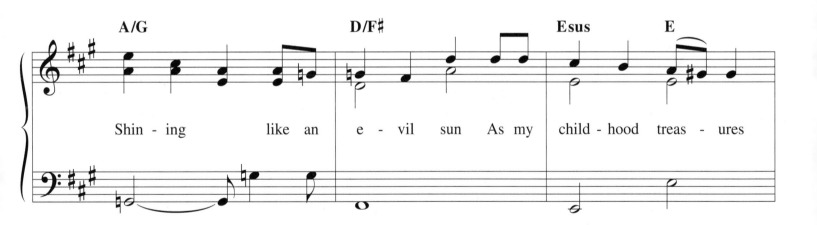

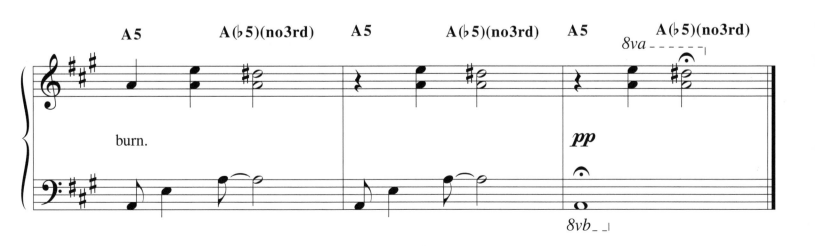

ANOTHER PYRAMID

Music by ELTON JOHN
Lyrics by TIM RICE

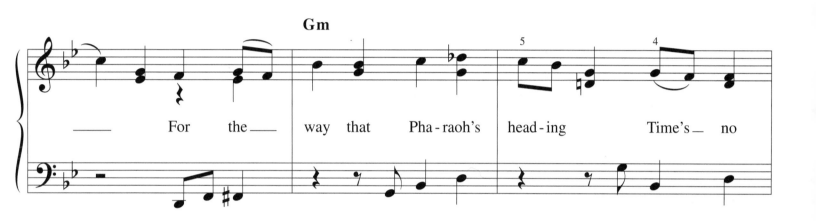

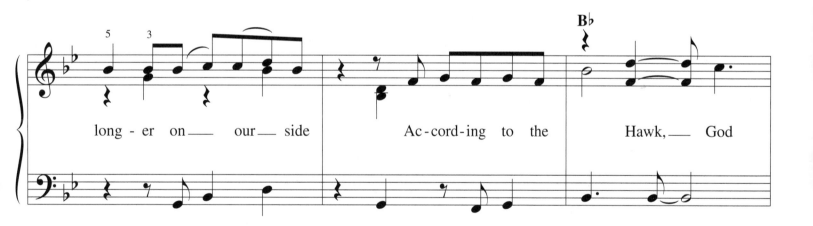

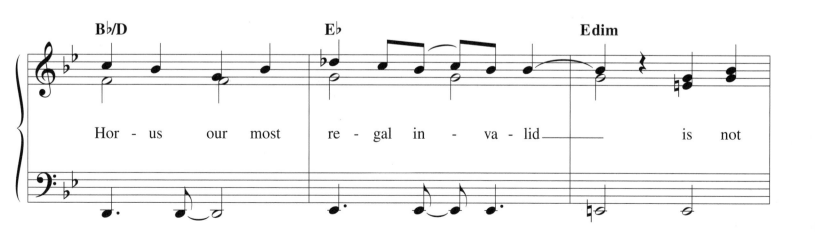

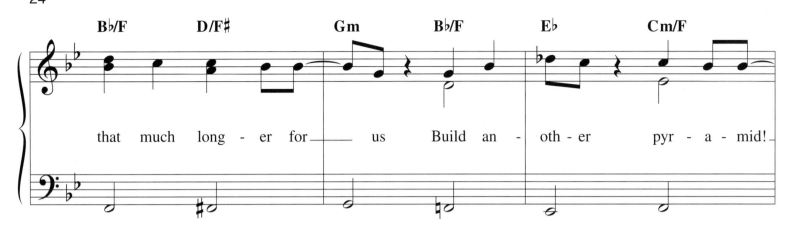

that much long - er for _____ us Build an - oth - er pyr - a - mid!

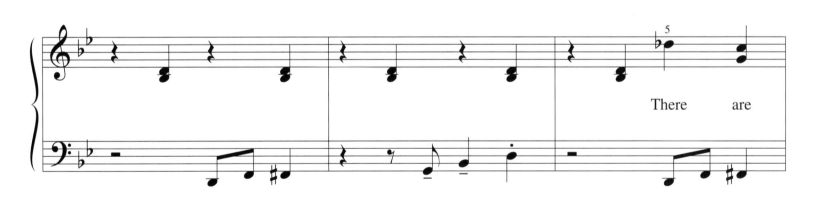

There are

man - y who'll be tear - ful As our lead - er fades ____ a - way ____

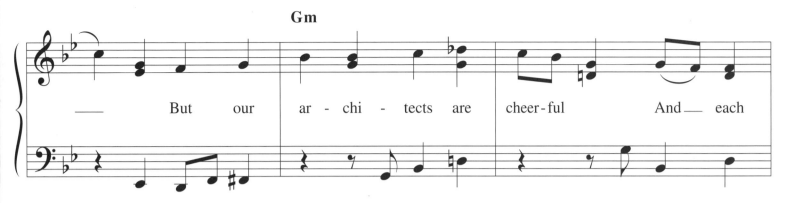

But our ar - chi - tects are cheer-ful And __ each

dog must have __ its day   If   our __ coun - try is __ to flour -

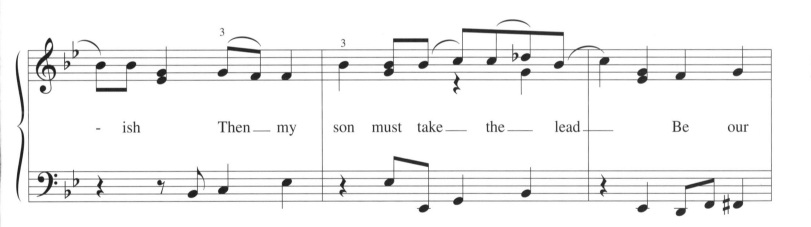

- ish   Then __ my   son must take __ the __ lead __   Be   our

in - spi - ra - tion, __ nour - ish   All our   hopes,   our   dreams, our creed __

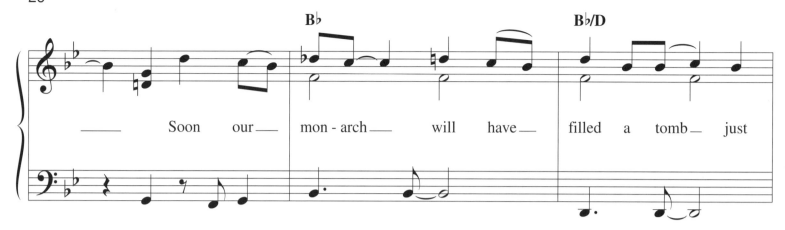

Soon our monarch will have filled a tomb just

like his fa - thers did____ Sum - mon E - gypt's great - est build -

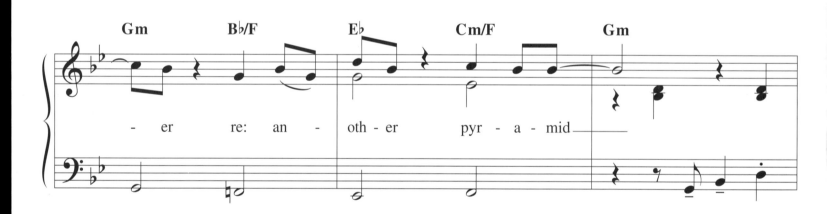

- er re: an - oth - er pyr - a - mid____

MINISTERS:

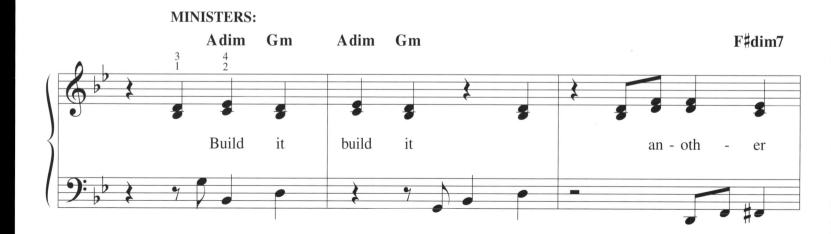

Build it build it an - oth - er

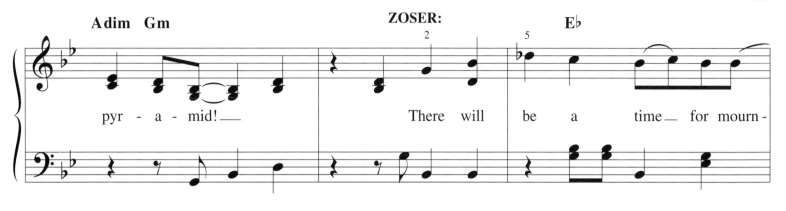

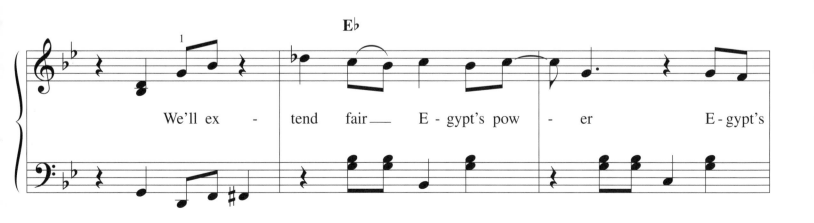

glo - ry strength and style ___ We shall have our fin - est hour ___

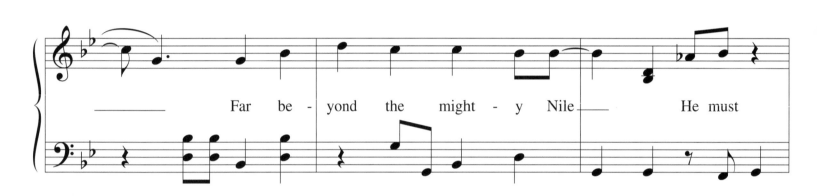

___ Far be - yond the might - y Nile ___ He must

have a vault ___ that's grand ___ by An - y stan - dards, floor ___ to lid ___

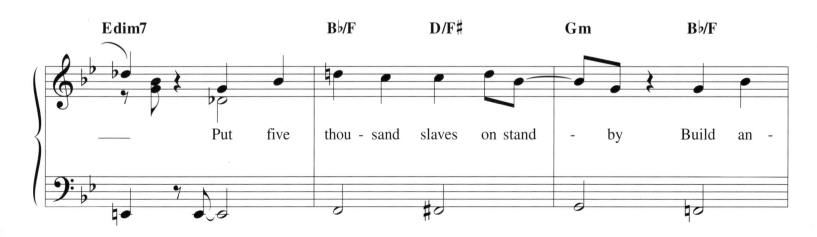

___ Put five thou - sand slaves on stand - by Build an -

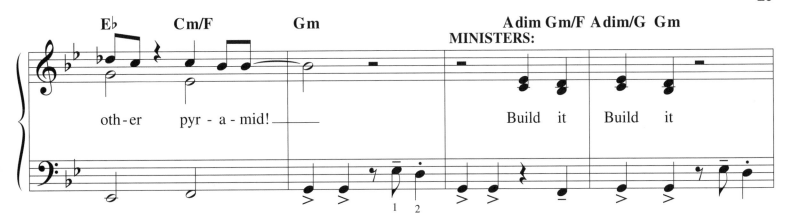

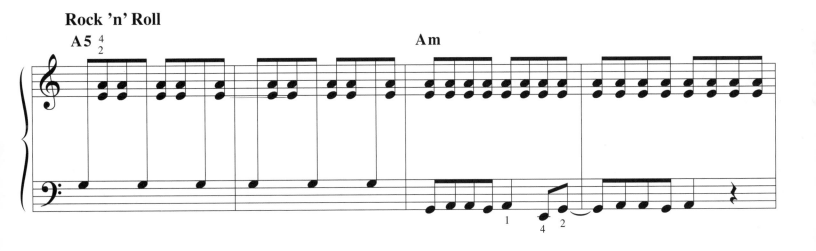

F7

F5   **Faster**

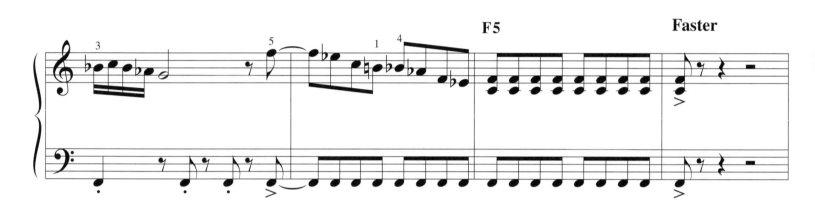

"Elbow Funk"

Am

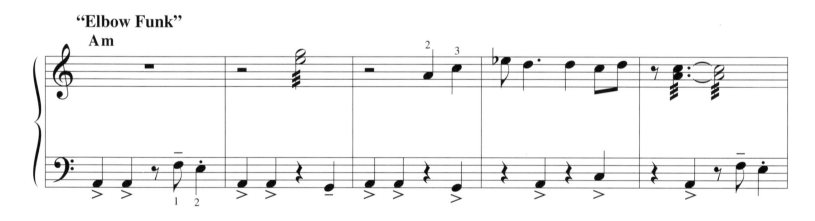

E♭5 D5   **C5 D5**   **Am**

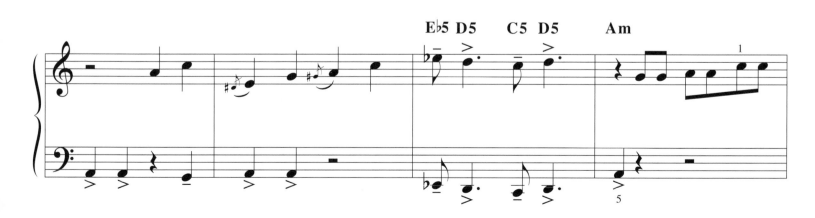

ZOSER:

He must have a vault that's grand by An - y

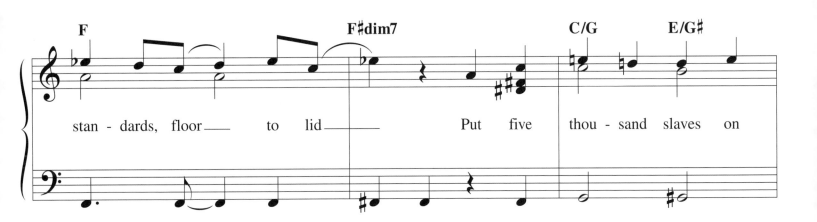

stan - dards, floor to lid Put five thou - sand slaves on

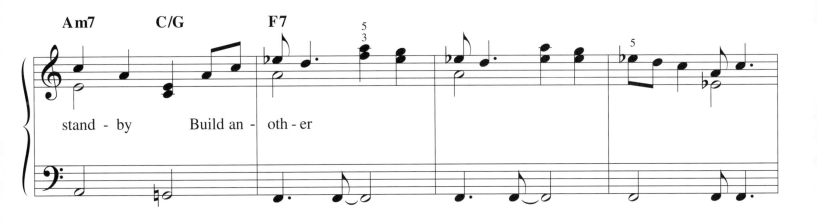

stand - by Build an - oth - er

pyr - a - mid!

HOW I KNOW YOU

Music by ELTON JOHN
Lyrics by TIM RICE

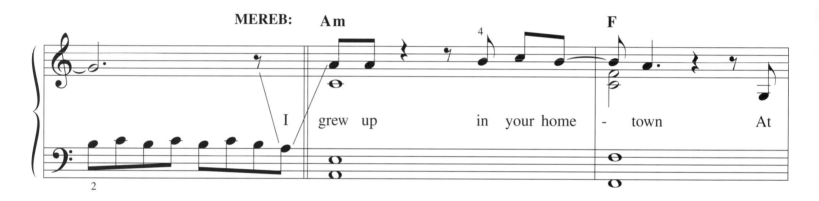

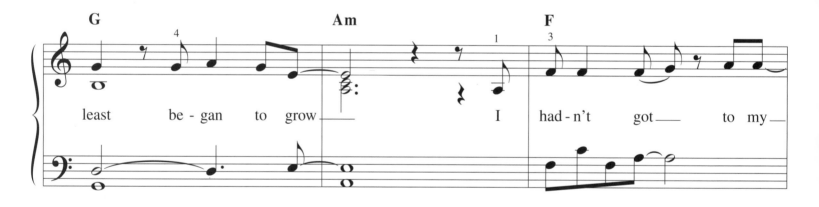

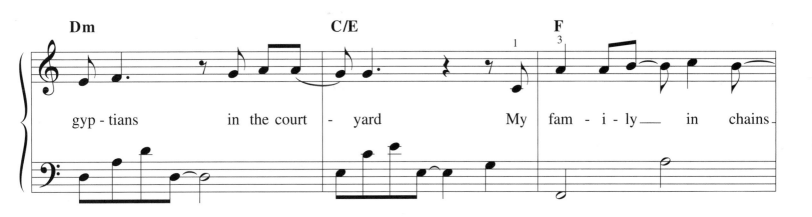

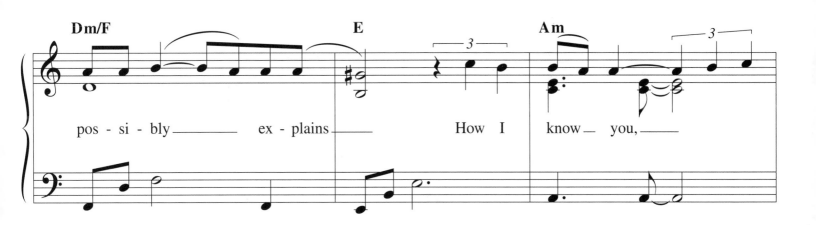

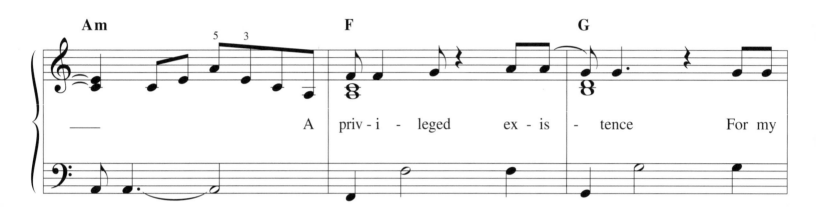

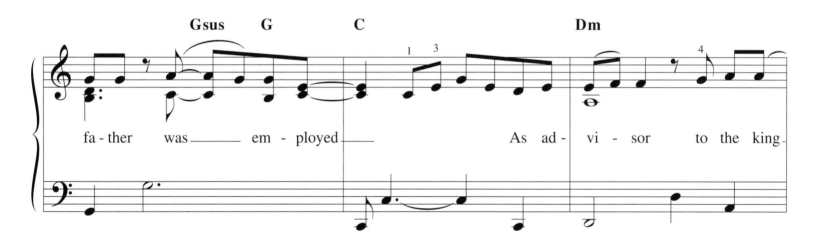

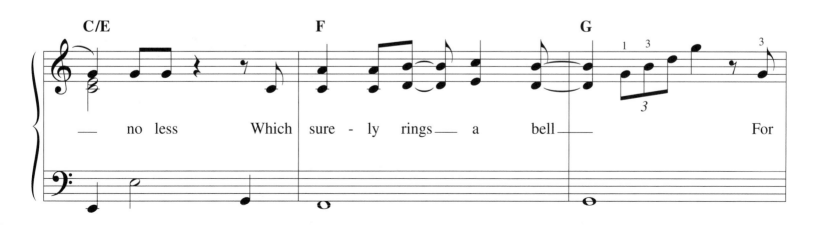

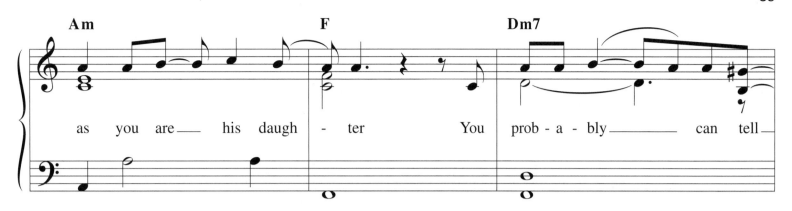

as you are— his daugh - ter You prob - a - bly——— can tell

— How I know—— you—— Yes I

know—— you You know too much and

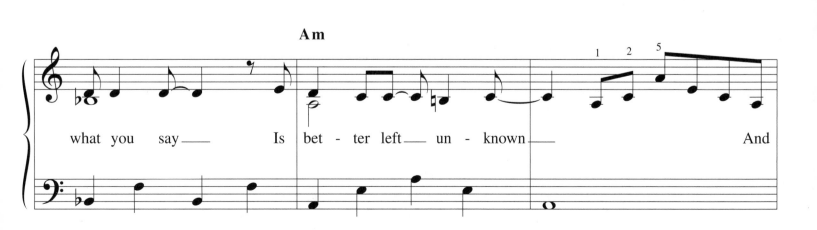

what you say— Is bet - ter left un - known— And

now I'm— just a slave— like you Our lives are not our own.

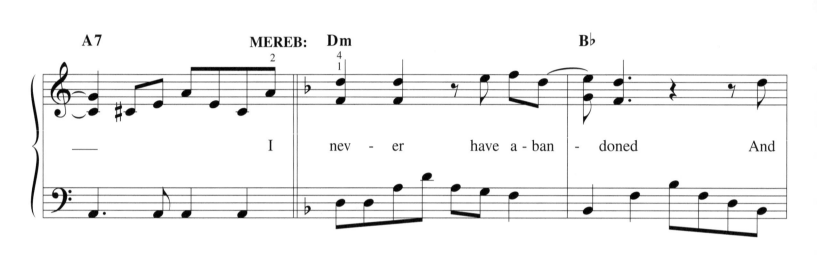

— I nev - er have a - ban - doned And

nor I think— could you That spark of hope— for free-

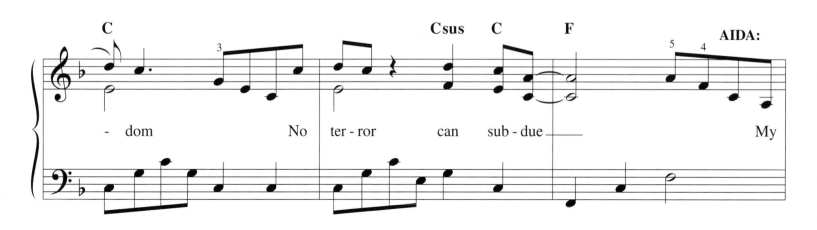

- dom No ter - ror can sub - due— My

38

know you___ You don't know me.___

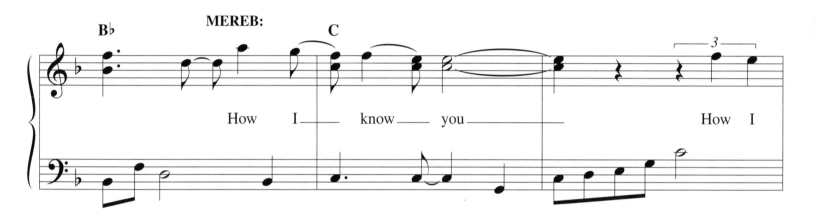

How I___ know___ you_____ How I

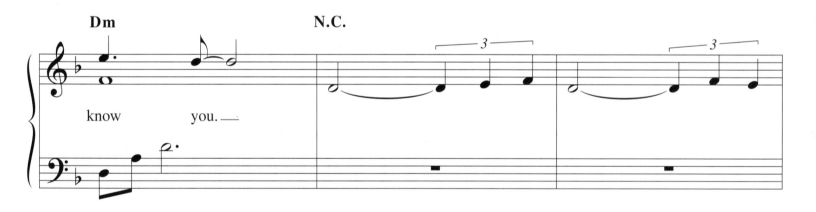

know you.___

MY STRONGEST SUIT

Music by ELTON JOHN
Lyrics by TIM RICE

Quasi recitative

AMNERIS:

In life one has to face a huge as-sort-ment Of nau-se-at-ing fads and good ad-vice. There's health and fit-ness, di-et and de-port-ment, And oth-er point-less forms of sac-ri-fice. Con-ver-sa-tion? Wit? I am a doubt-er. Man-ners? Charm? They're no way to impress.

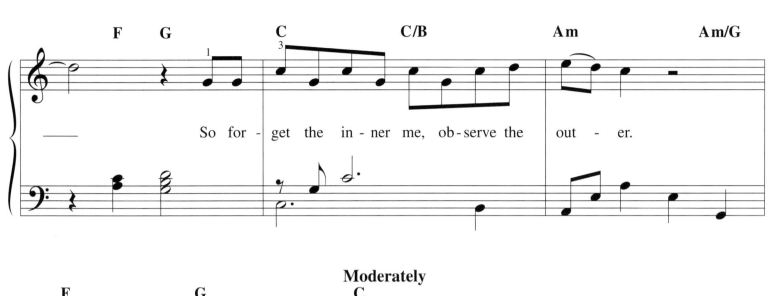

So for-get the in-ner me, ob-serve the out - er.

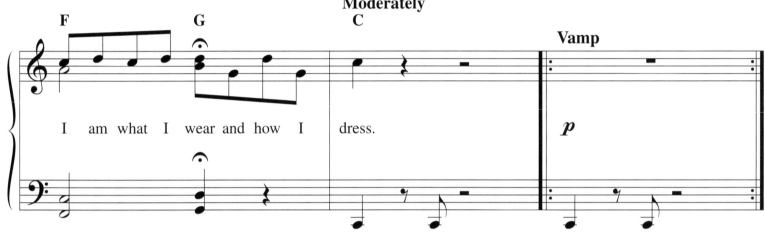

Moderately

I am what I wear and how I dress.

Vamp

Oh,— now I— be-lieve— in look - ing like my

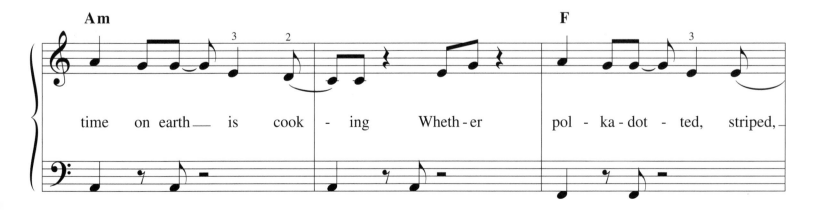

time on earth— is cook - ing Wheth-er pol-ka-dot-ted, striped,

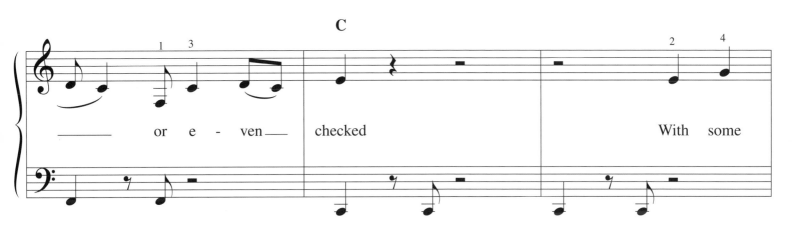

or e - ven checked With some

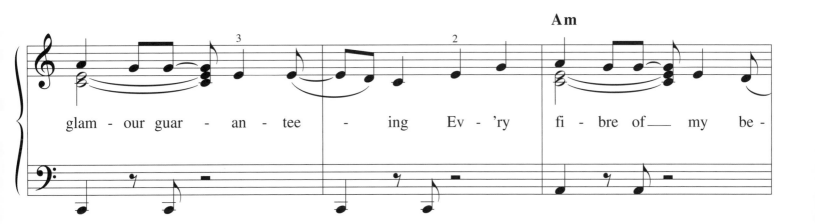

glam - our guar - an - tee - ing Ev - 'ry fi - bre of my be -

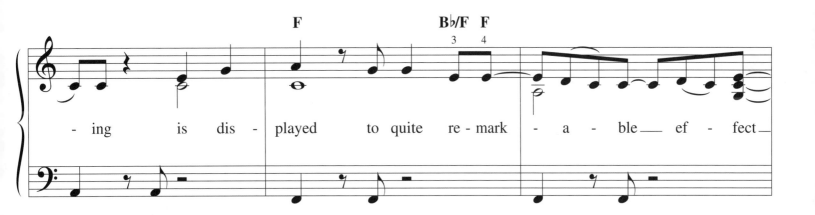

- ing is dis - played to quite re - mark - a - ble ef - fect

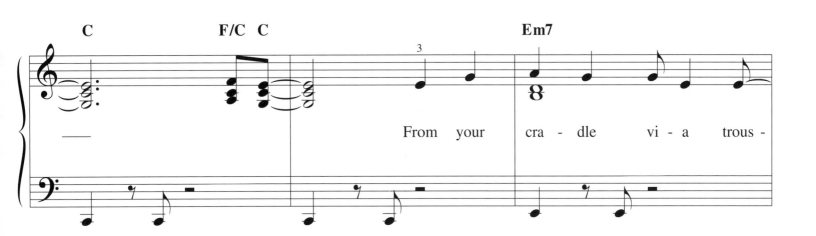

From your cra - dle vi - a trous -

- seau,___ to your death - bed you're on view,___ so nev-er com-

- pro - mise,___ ac - cept no sub - sti - tute_____

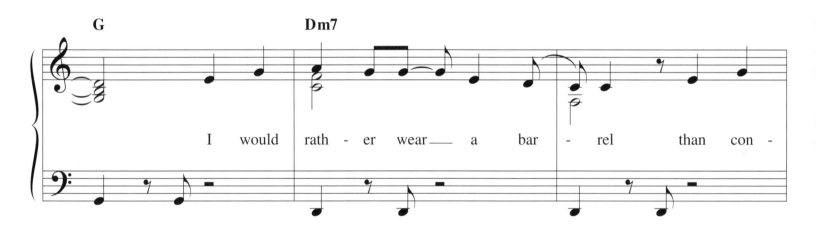

I would rath - er wear___ a bar - rel than con-

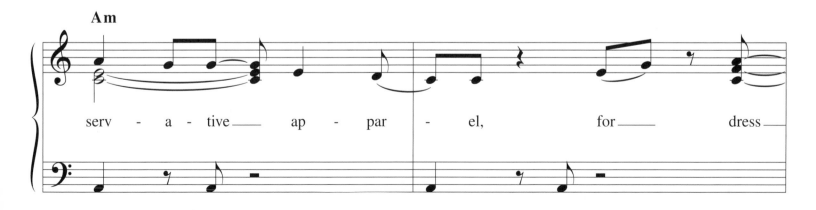

serv - a - tive___ ap - par - el, for___ dress

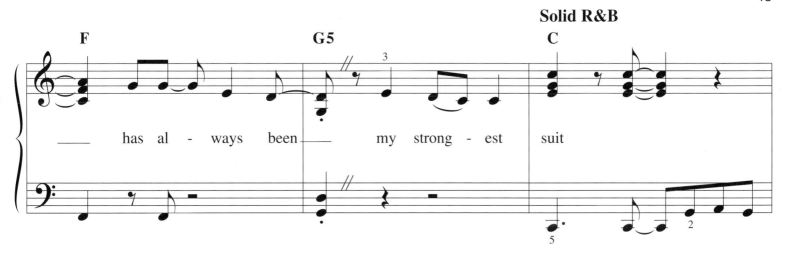

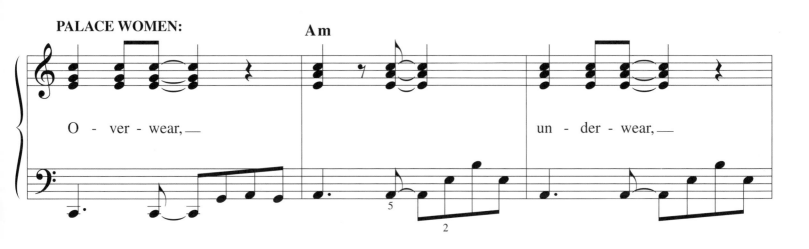

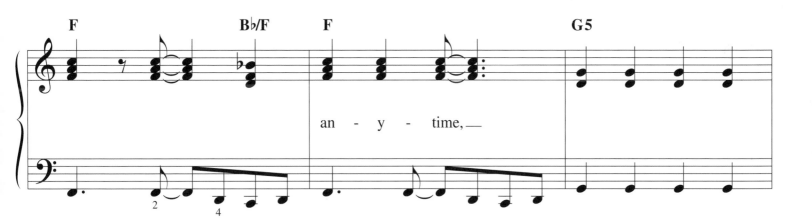

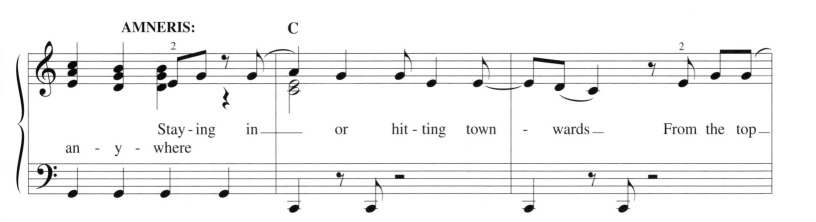

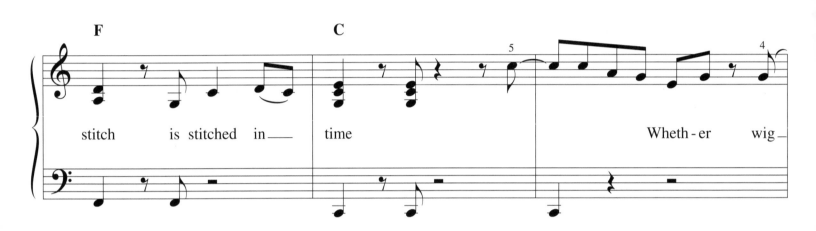

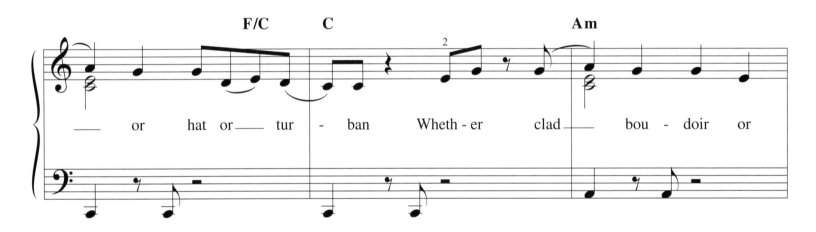

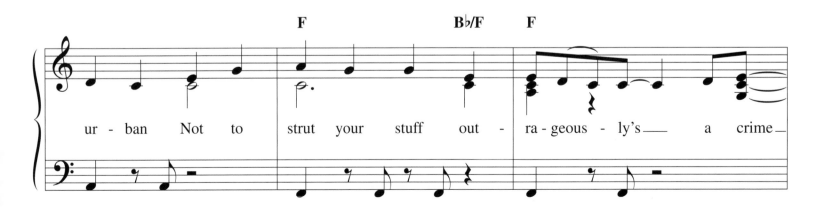

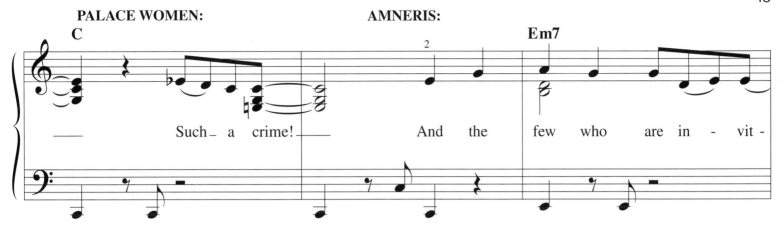

PALACE WOMEN: **AMNERIS:**

Such a crime! And the few who are in-vit-

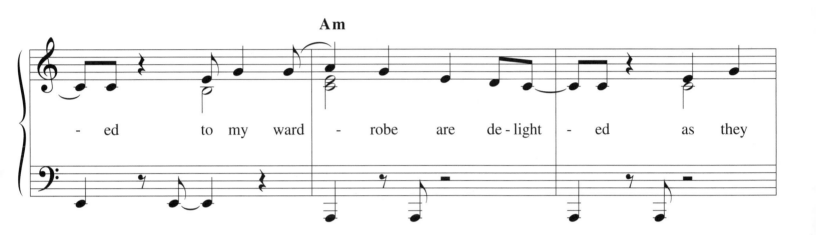

-ed to my ward-robe are de-light-ed as they

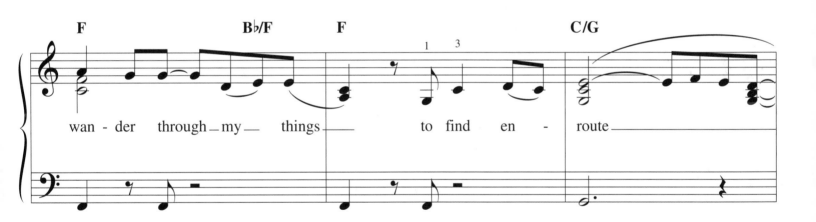

wan-der through my things to find en-route

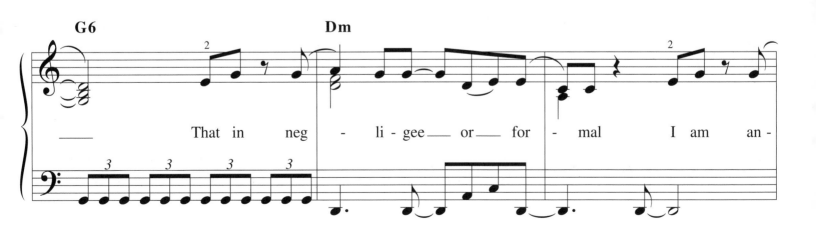

That in neg-li-gee or for-mal I am an-

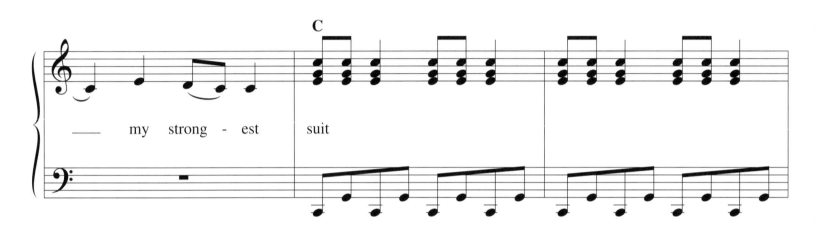

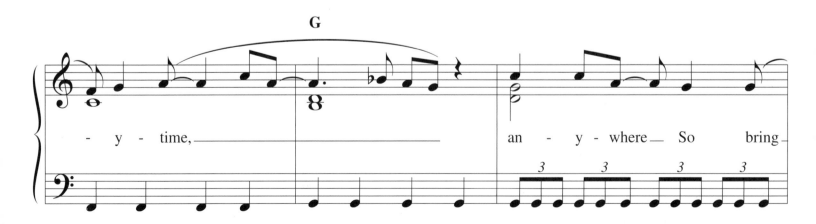

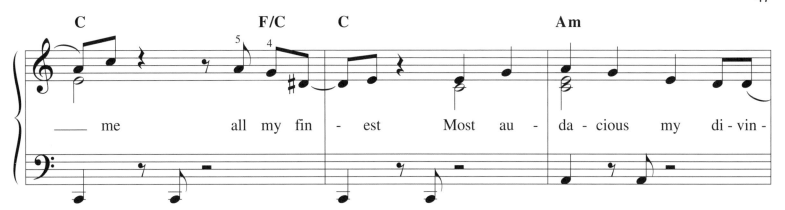

_____ me all my fin - est Most au - da - cious my di - vin-

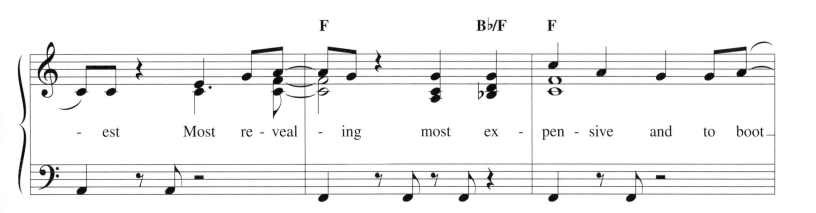

- est Most re - veal - ing most ex - pen - sive and to boot____

_____ Most ar - rest -

- ing, most___ heart - stop-ping Most free -

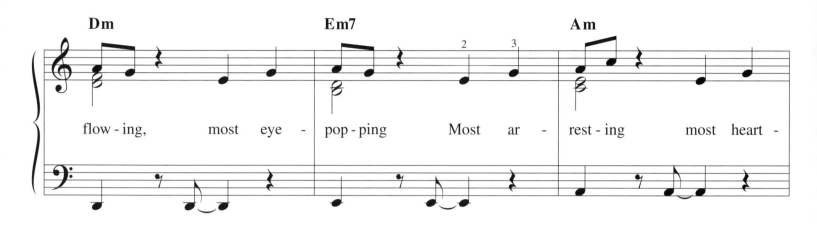

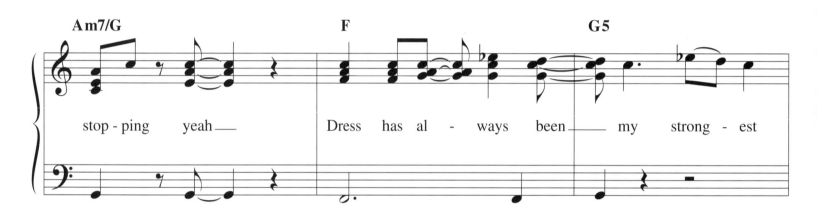

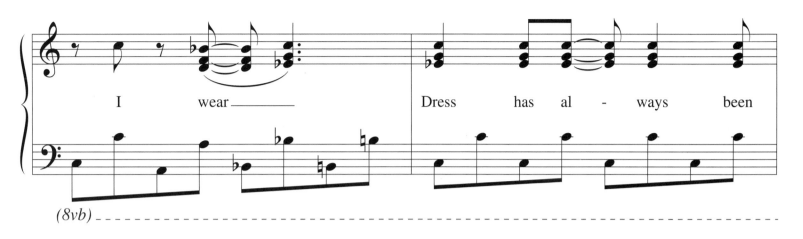

I wear _____ Dress has al - ways been

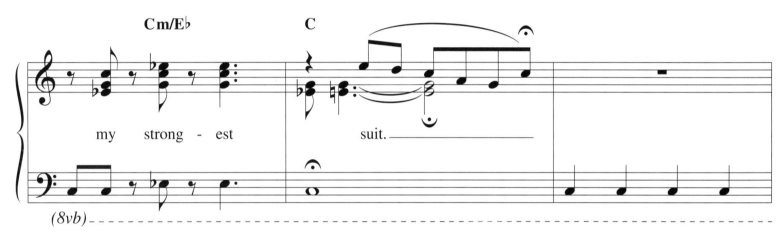

Cm/E♭ **C**

my strong - est suit. _____

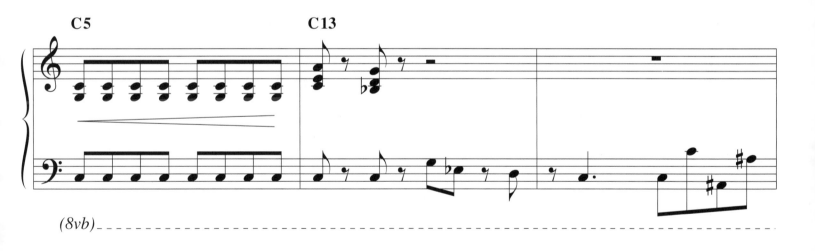

C5 **C13**

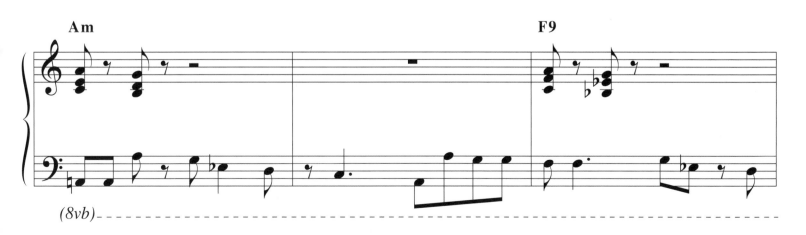

Am **F9**

50

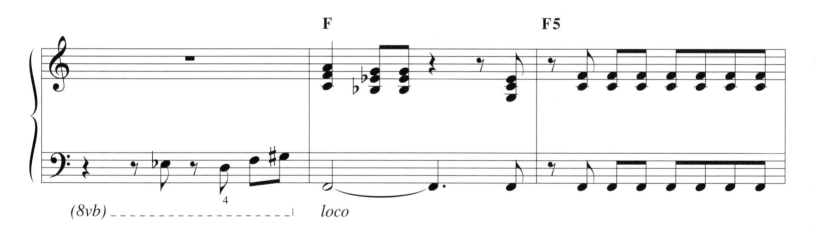

C7#9

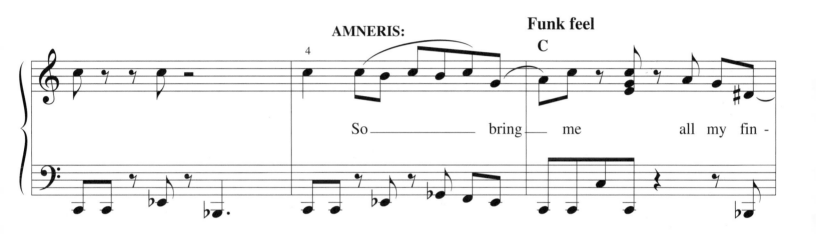

AMNERIS: **Funk feel** **C**

So _____ bring ___ me ___ all my fin -

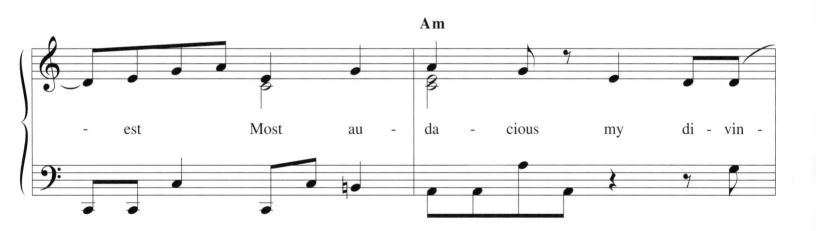

Am

- est Most au - da - cious my di - vin -

F

- est Most re - veal - ing, most ex -

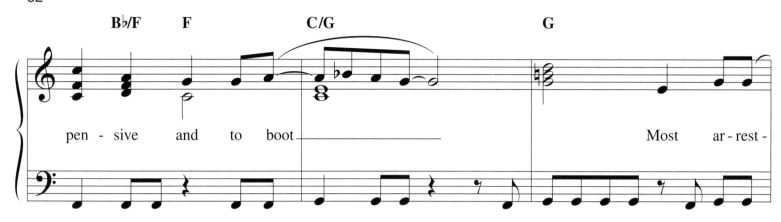

pen - sive and to boot _____ Most ar - rest -

- ing, most heart - stop-ping most free - flow-ing most_ eye -

pop - ping Dress has al - ways been_ my strong - est

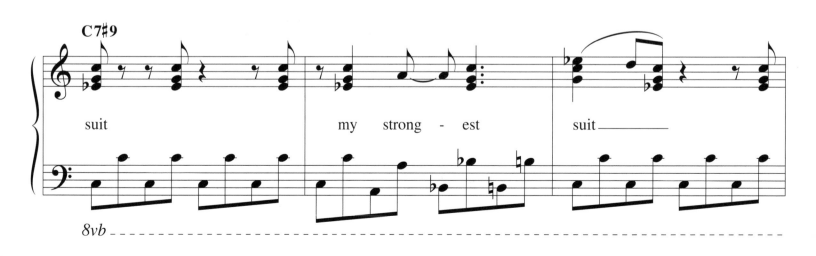

suit my strong - est suit _____

8vb -

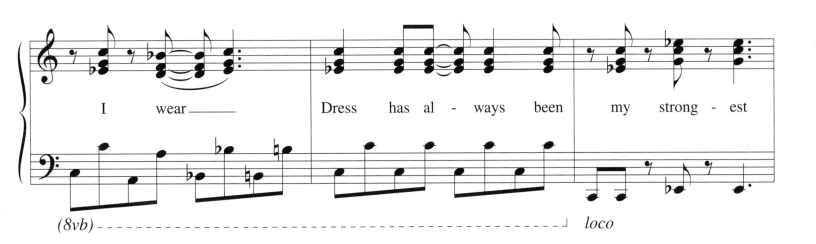

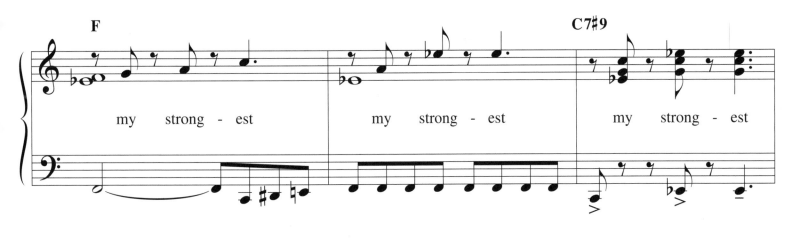

ENCHANTMENT PASSING THROUGH

Music by ELTON JOHN
Lyrics by TIM RICE

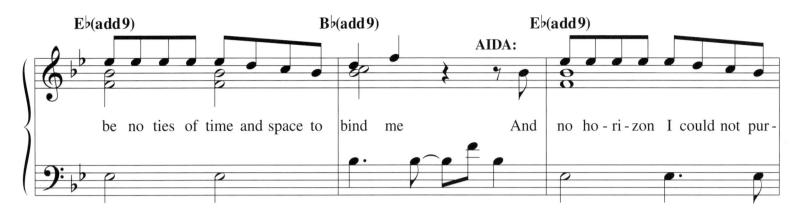

be no ties of time and space to bind me   And   no ho - ri - zon I could not pur-

sue   I'd   leave the world's mis - for - tunes far be - hind me   I'd

put my faith and trust in some - thing new   But why   should I

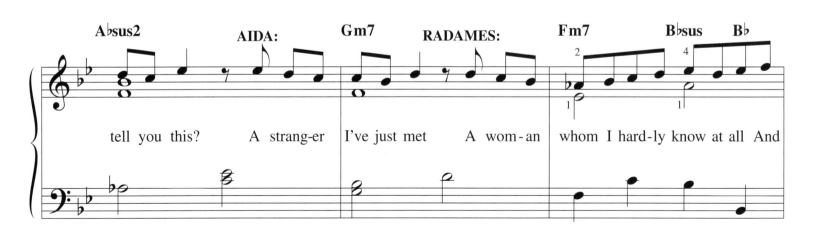

tell you this?   A strang - er   I've just met   A wom - an   whom I hard - ly know at all And

should for-get   A jour-ney   we can on-ly dream of_____   En-chant-ment pass-ing

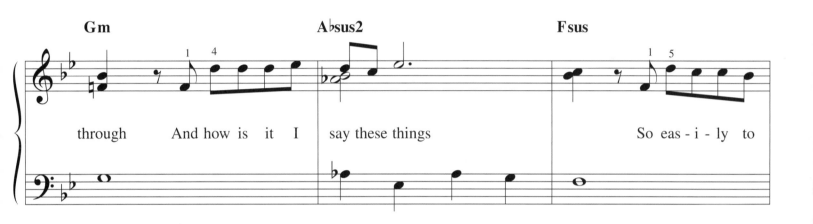

through   And how is it I   say these things   So eas-i-ly to

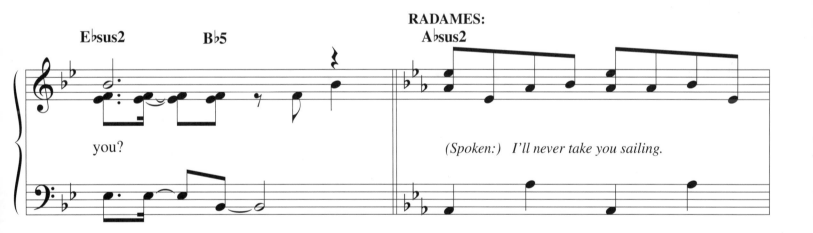

you?   *(Spoken:) I'll never take you sailing.*

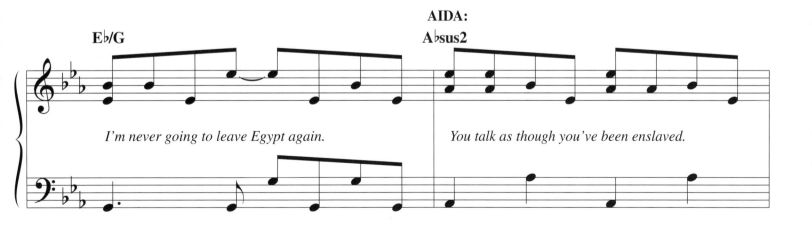

I'm never going to leave Egypt again.   *You talk as though you've been enslaved.*

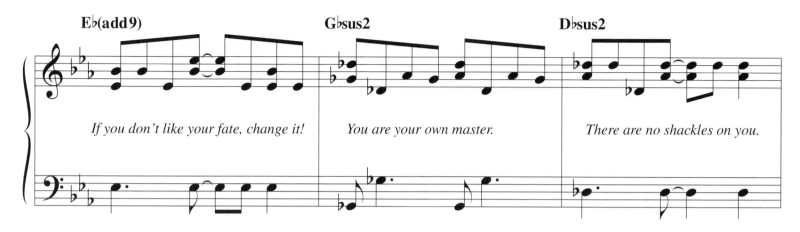

If you don't like your fate, change it! You are your own master. There are no shackles on you.

So don't expect any pity, or understanding, from this humble palace slave. But

why   did I   tell her this?   A strang-er   I've just met   A wom-an

whom I hard-ly know at all and   will for-get   A-non-y-mous and gone to-mor - row

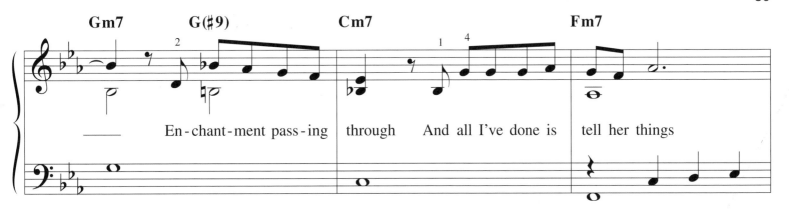

Gm7 G(#9) Cm7 Fm7

En-chant-ment pass-ing through And all I've done is tell her things

D♭(add9) B♭sus A♭sus2 E♭sus2 A♭sus2 E♭sus2(add4)

She al-read-y knew

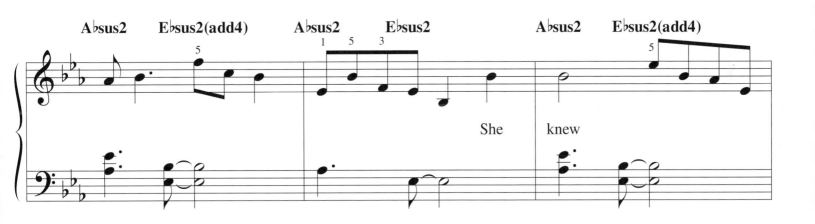

A♭sus2 E♭sus2(add4) A♭sus2 E♭sus2 A♭sus2 E♭sus2(add4)

She knew

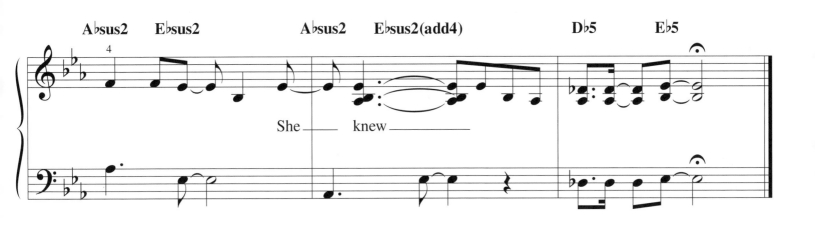

A♭sus2 E♭sus2 A♭sus2 E♭sus2(add4) D♭5 E♭5

She knew

DANCE OF THE ROBE

Music by ELTON JOHN
Lyrics by TIM RICE

Dictated, in 1

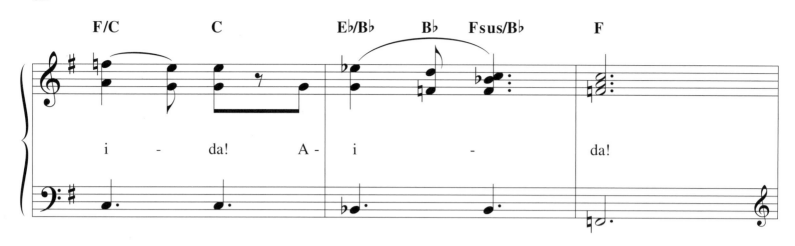

i - da! A - i - da!

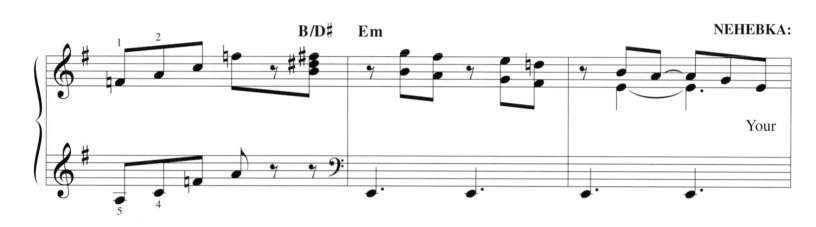

NEHEBKA:

Your

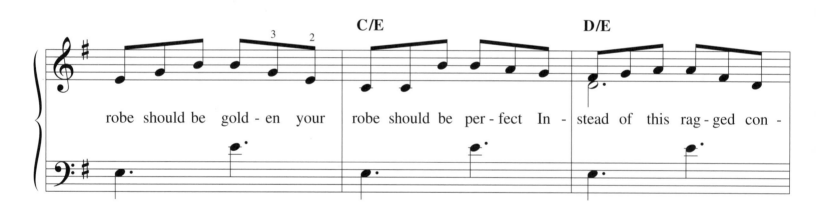

robe should be gold - en your robe should be per - fect In - stead of this rag - ged con -

coc - tion of thread But may you be moved by its des - per - ate beau - ty To

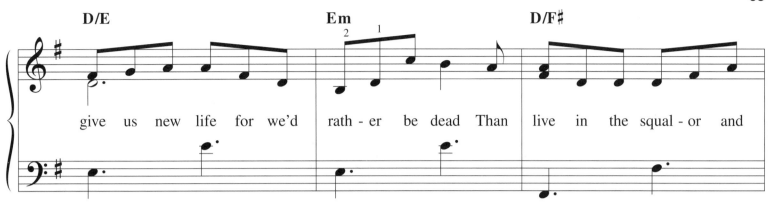

give us new life for we'd rath-er be dead Than live in the squal-or and

shame of the slave To the dance! To the dance!

NUBIANS:

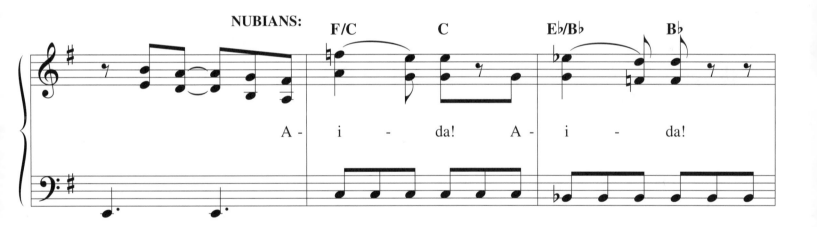

A - i - da! A - i - da!

All we ask of you All we ask Is a life-time of serv-ice,

64

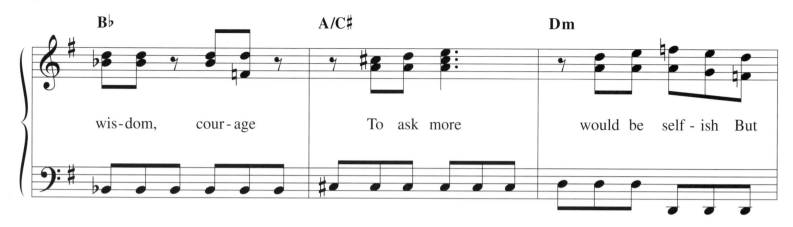

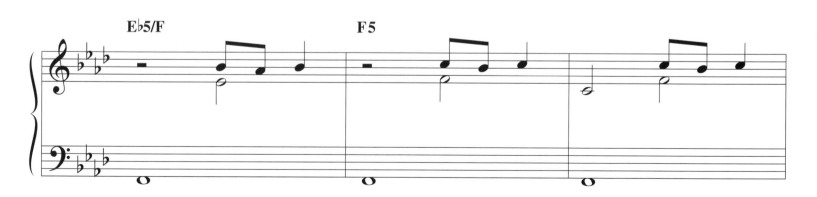

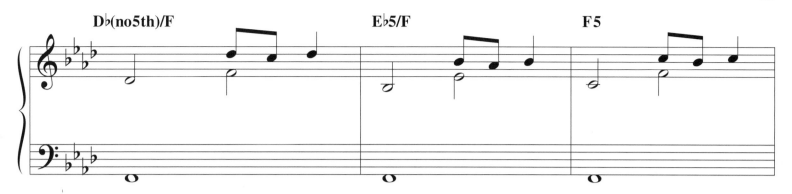

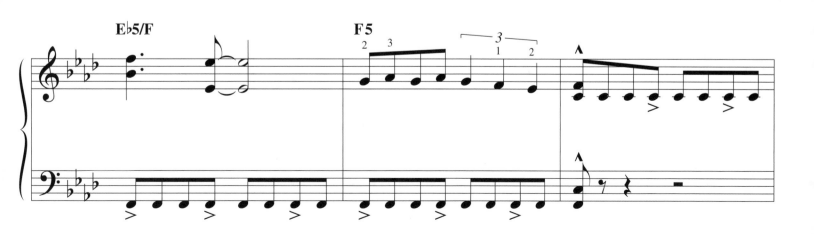

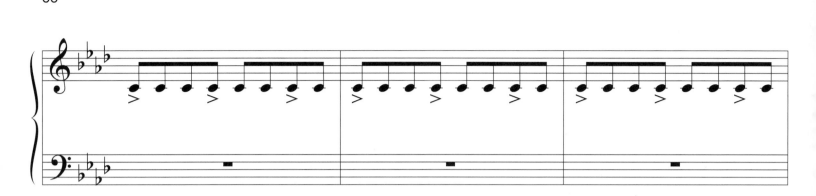

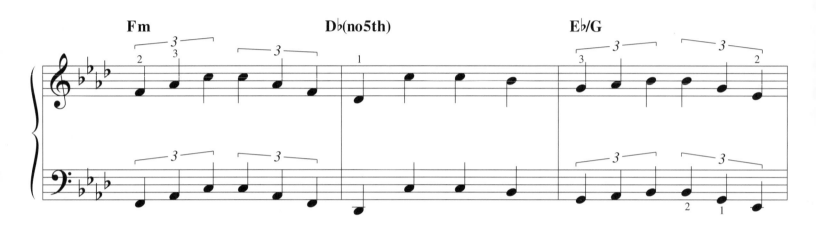

A - i - da! A-

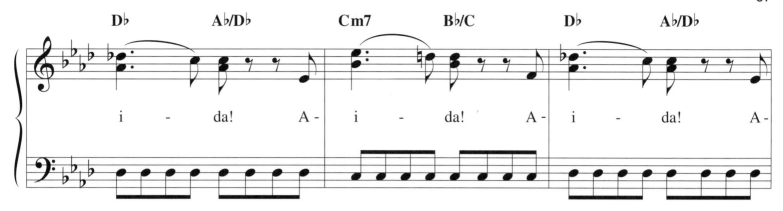

i - da! A - i - da! A - i - da! A-

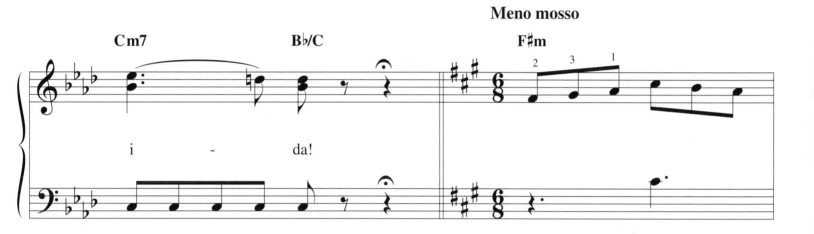

i - da!

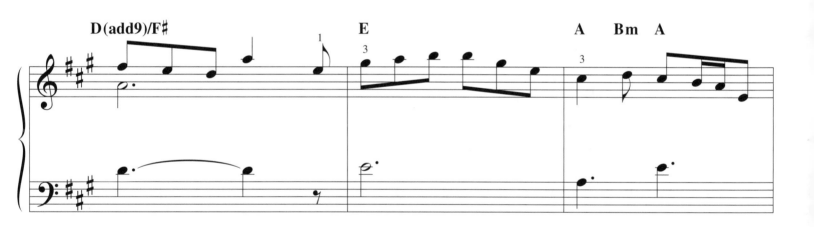

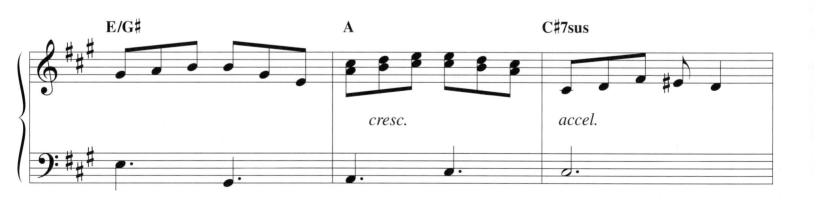

A tempo

AIDA:

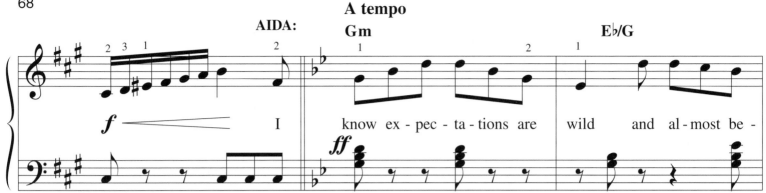

I know ex - pec - ta - tions are wild and al - most be -

yond my ful - fill - ment but they won't hear A word of a doubt or see

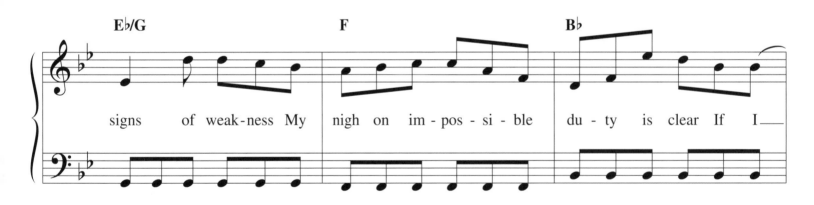

signs of weak - ness My nigh on im - pos - si - ble du - ty is clear If I___

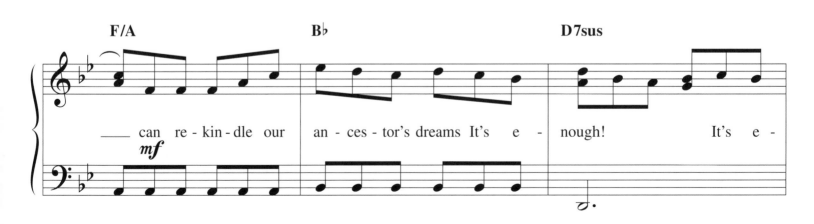

___ can re - kin - dle our an - ces - tor's dreams It's e - nough! It's e -

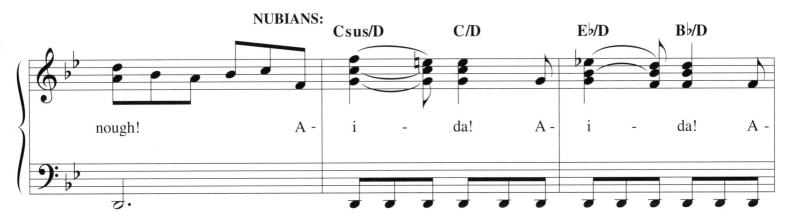

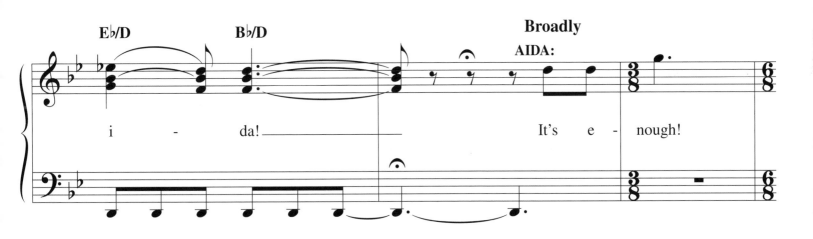

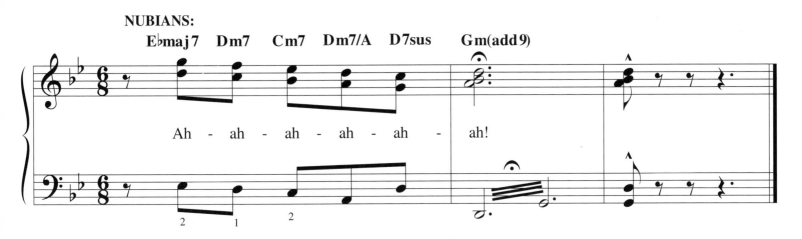

NOT ME

Music by ELTON JOHN
Lyrics by TIM RICE

Not me _____ Who'd have guessed I'd throw my world_ a - way?_ To

be with some-one I'm a-fraid____ will say____ "Not me?"___ This can nev - er

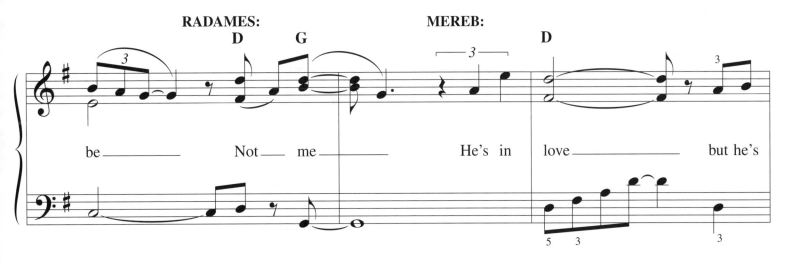

be _____ Not__ me_____ He's in love_____ but he's

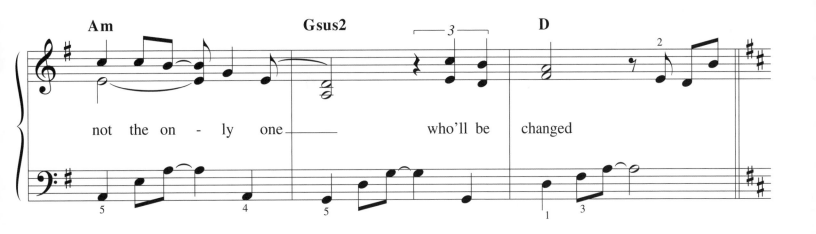

not the on - ly one__ who'll be changed

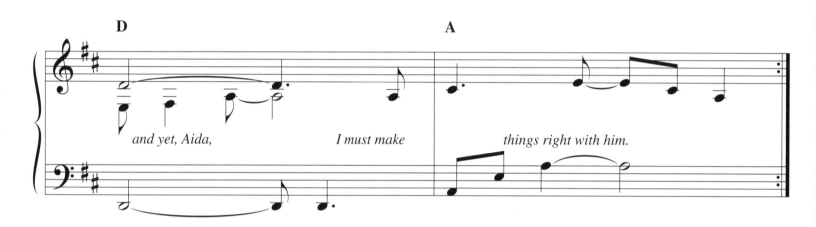

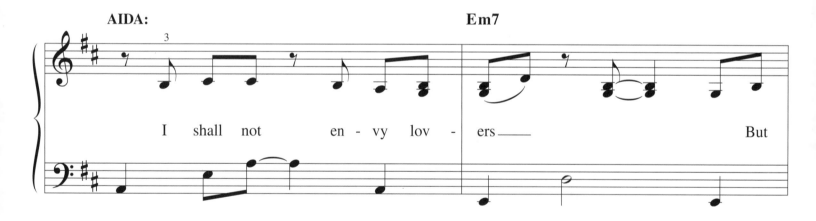

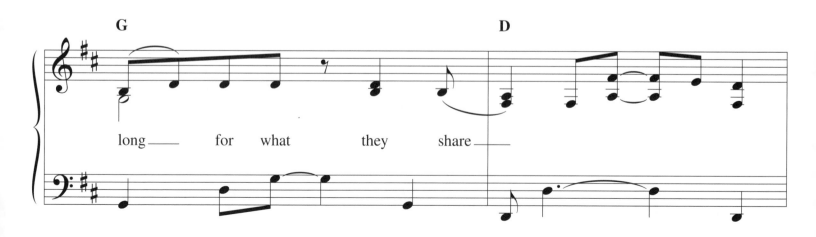

AMNERIS:

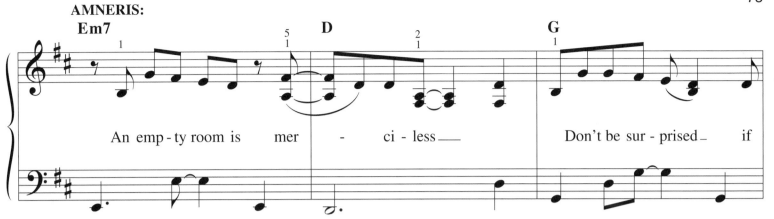

An emp - ty room is mer - - ci - less — Don't be sur - prised — if

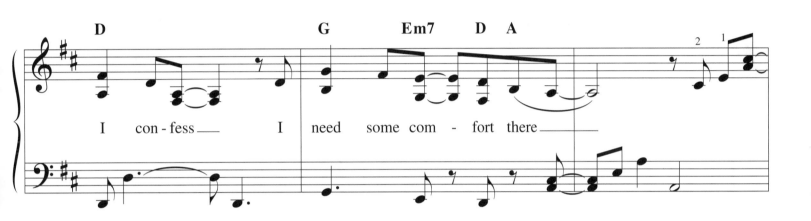

I con - fess — I need some com - fort there —

AIDA & AMNERIS:

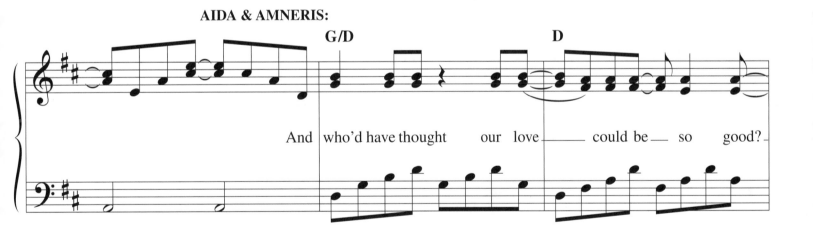

And who'd have thought our love — could be — so good? —

Not me — Not me — And

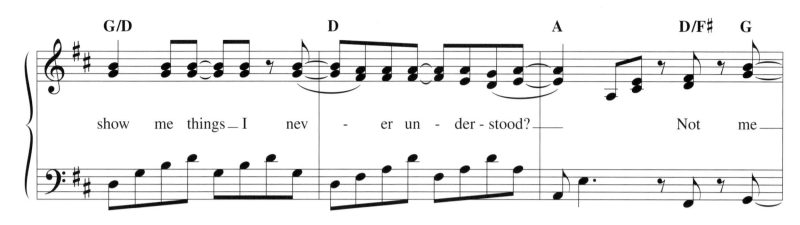

show me things — I nev - er un - der - stood? — Not me —

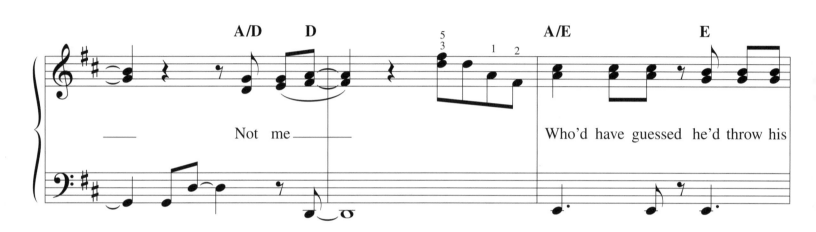

— Not me — Who'd have guessed he'd throw his

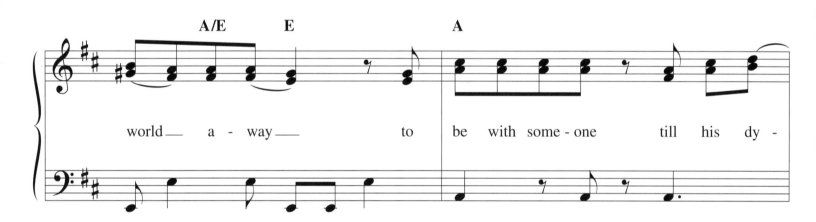

world — a - way — to be with some-one till his dy -

- ing day? — Not me — Not me.

Who'd have guessed I'd throw my world — a - way — To
(he'd) (his)

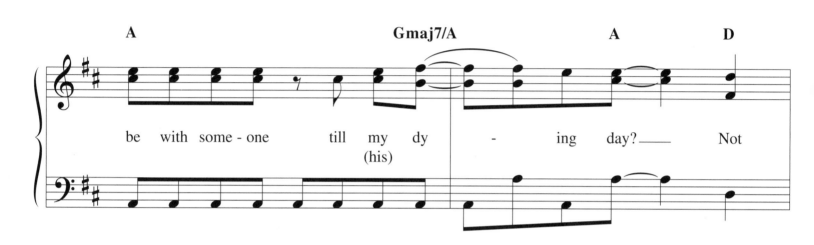

be with some - one till my dy - ing day? — Not
(his)

me Not me —

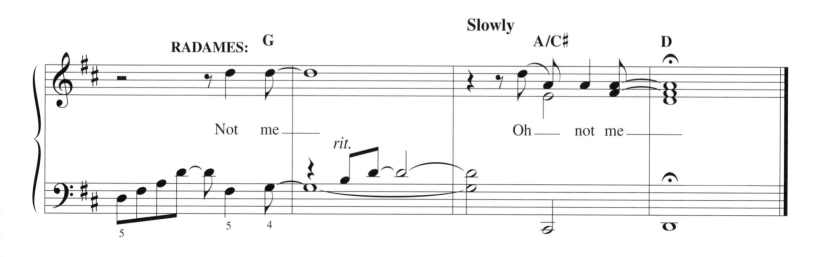

RADAMES:
Not me — Oh — not me —

ELABORATE LIVES

Music by ELTON JOHN
Lyrics by TIM RICE

Moderately, with rubato

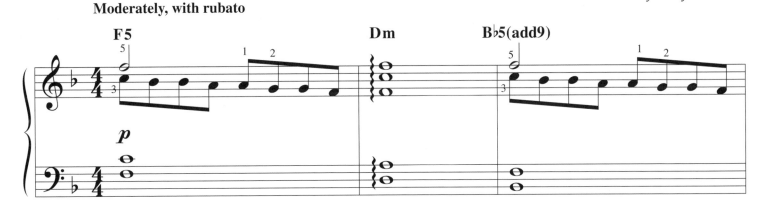

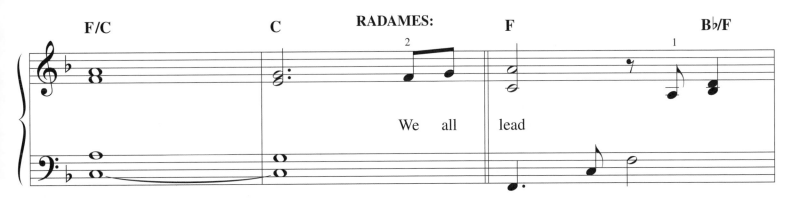

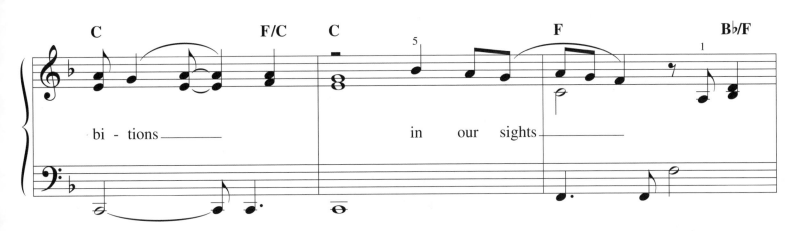

How an af - fair _____ of the heart sur - vives _

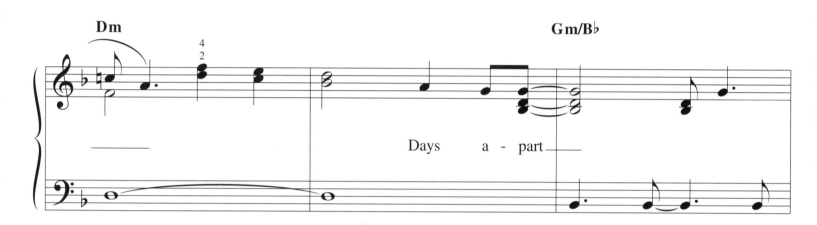

_____ Days a - part _____

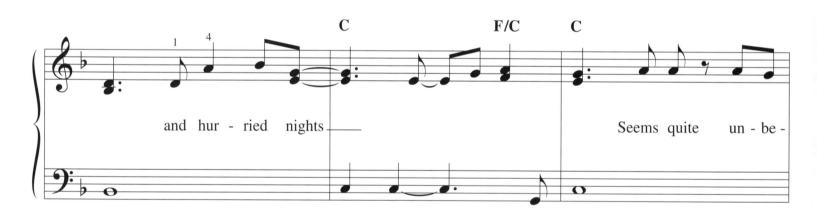

and hur - ried nights _____ Seems quite un - be -

With strict rhythm

liev - a - ble to me I don't want to live like that

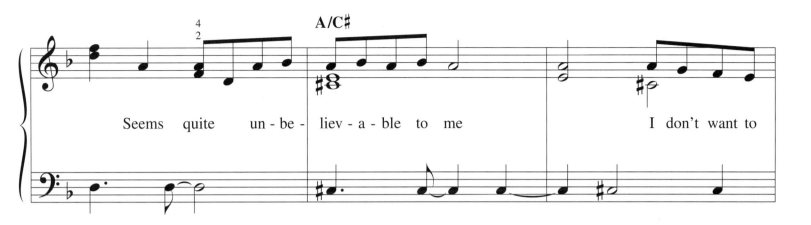

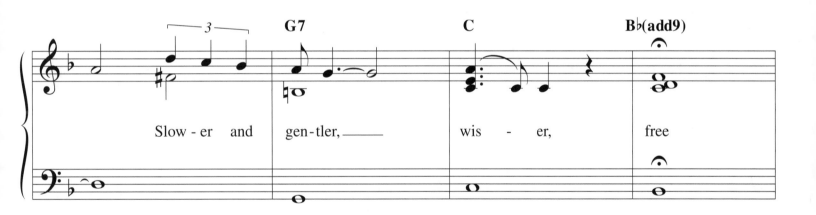

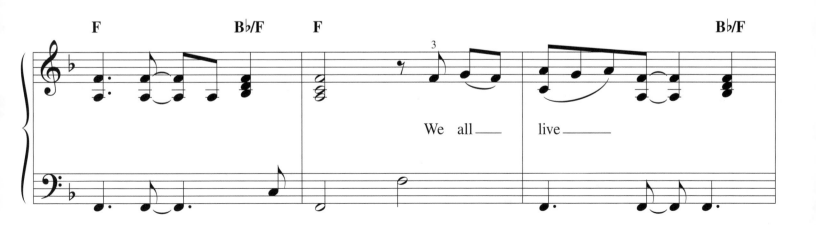

I'm so tired — of all —— we're go-ing through   I —— don't want to

live like that   I'm so tired —— of   all we're go-ing through

I don't want to love like that   I just want to be   with you —

—   Now and for - ev-er,   peace - ful,

true _____ This may not be the mo-ment

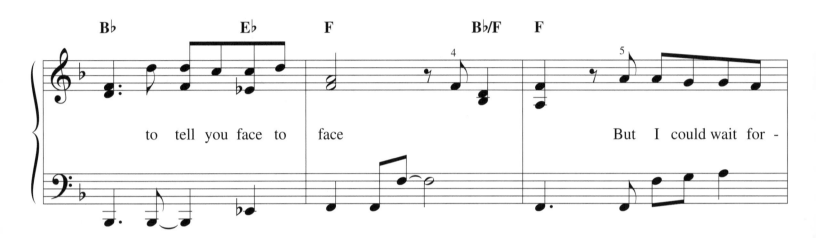

to tell you face to face But I could wait for -

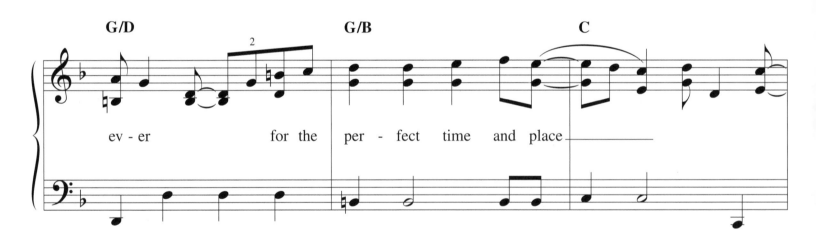

ev - er for the per - fect time and place _____

RADAMES & AIDA:

We all lead such e-lab-o-rate lives _____

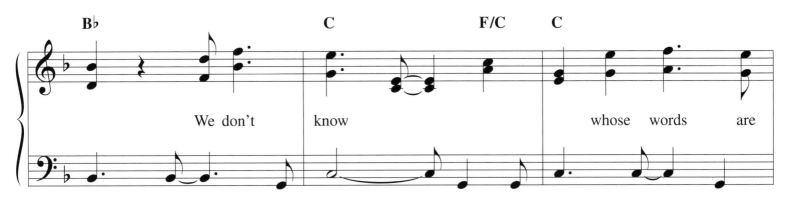

We don't know whose words are

true ___ Strang-ers, lov-ers, hus - bands,

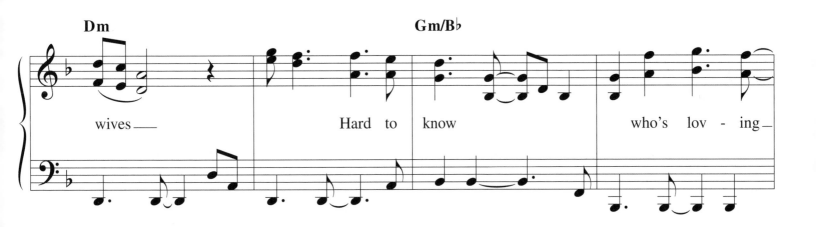

wives ___ Hard to know who's lov - ing ___

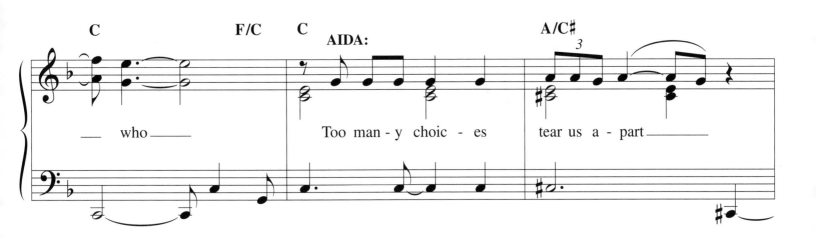

___ who ___ **AIDA:** Too man - y choic - es tear us a - part ___

86

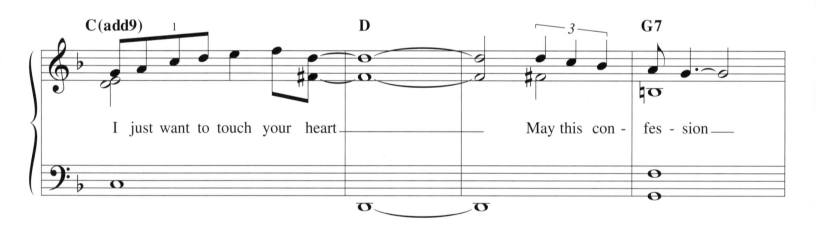

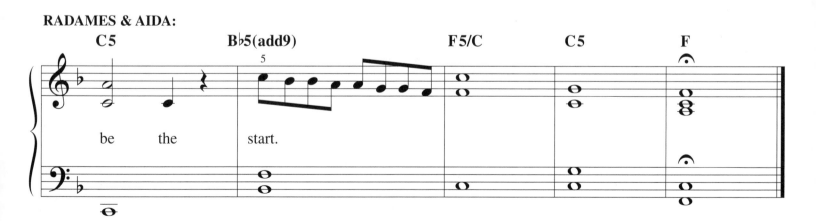

THE GODS LOVE NUBIA

Music by ELTON JOHN
Lyrics by TIM RICE

Measured, with inner strength

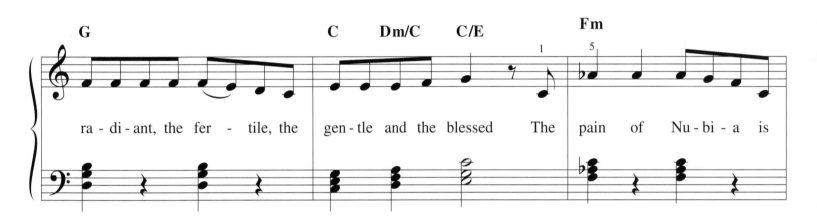

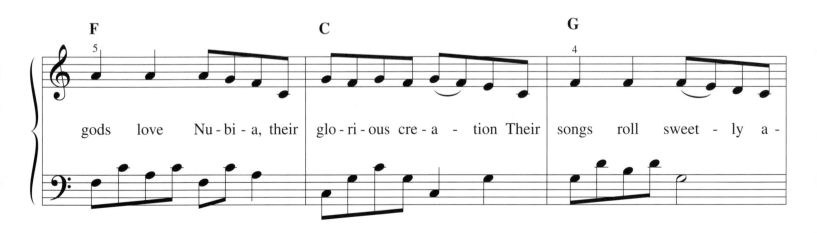

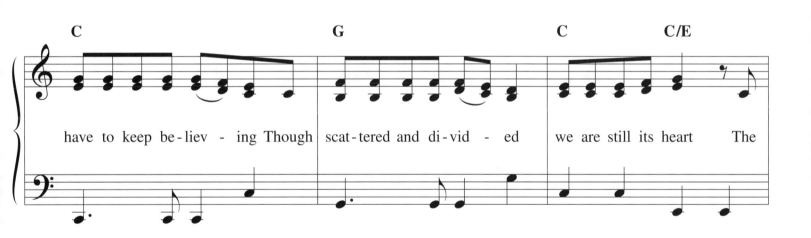

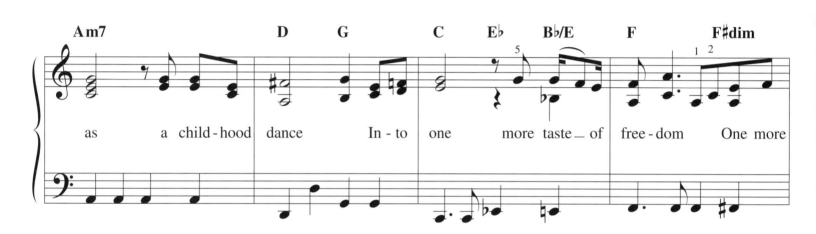

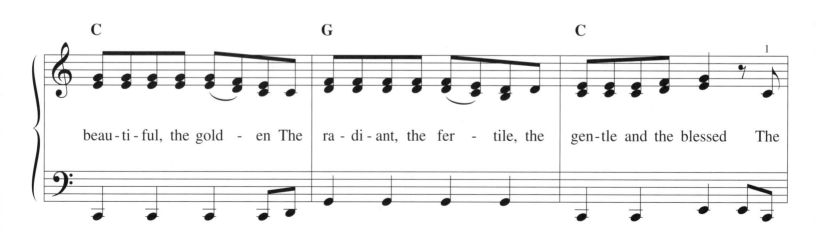

pain of Nu - bi - a is on - ly of the mo - ment The des - o - late, the suf - fer - ing, the

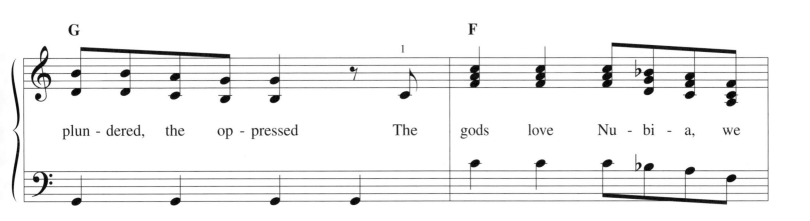

plun - dered, the op - pressed The gods love Nu - bi - a, we

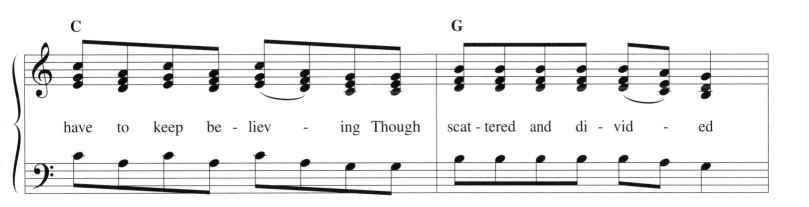

have to keep be - liev - ing Though scat - tered and di - vid - ed

we are still its heart The fall of Nu - bi - a, e -

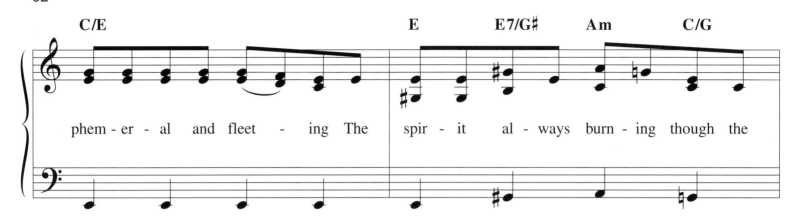

phem - er - al and fleet - ing The spir - it al - ways burn - ing though the

flesh is torn a - part The spir-it al-ways burn-ing though the flesh is torn ____ a -

AIDA:

Freely   **In tempo**

NEHEBKA & NUBIANS:

ALL:

part _____ Take me in my dreams re - cur - ring One more

rit.

Broadly

long - ing back - ward glance.

A STEP TOO FAR

Music by ELTON JOHN
Lyrics by TIM RICE

Moderately fast

It's so strange _____ he does-n't show _____ me More af - fec - tion than he needs

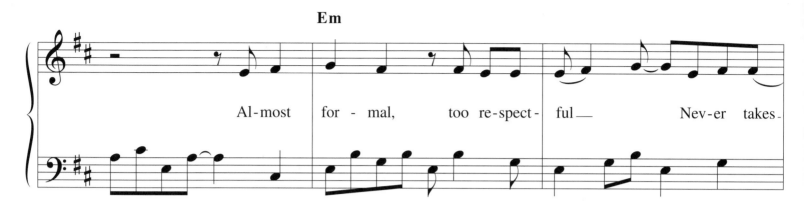

Al-most for - mal, too re-spect- ful — Nev-er takes

— ro - man-tic leads There are times when I i - mag -

ine — I'm not al - ways on his mind He's not

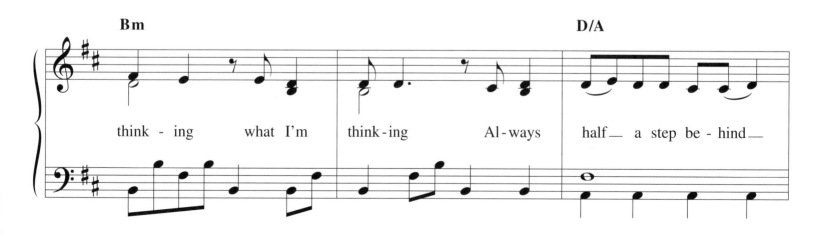

think - ing what I'm think-ing Al-ways half — a step be-hind —

Al-ways   half— a step be-hind   O—

_____ ho —   O_____ ho ——

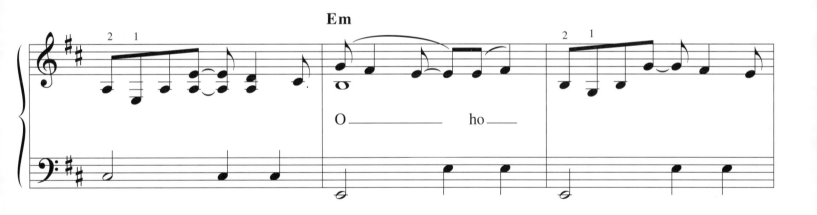

O_____ ho ——

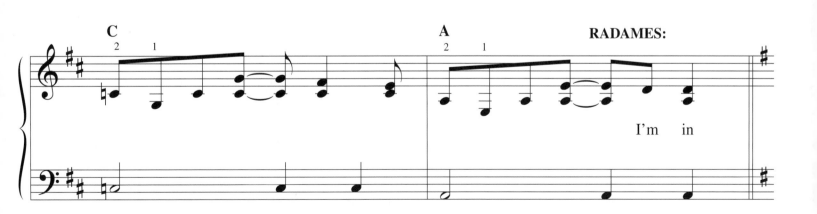

RADAMES:

I'm in

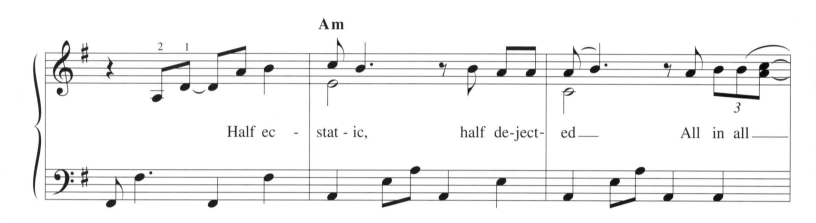

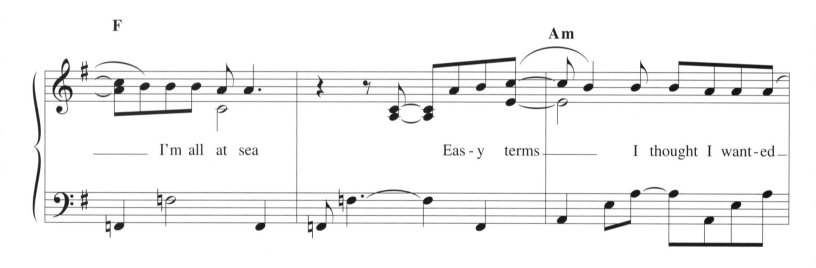

nev - er know the cha-os Of a life turned on its head

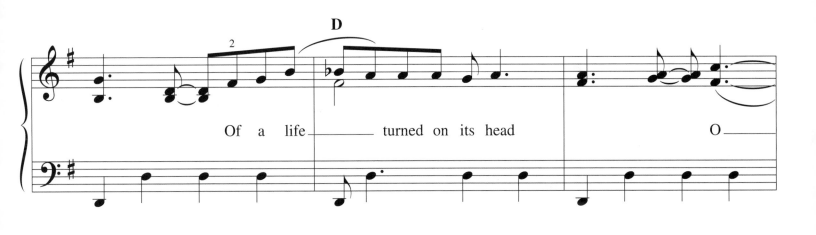

Of a life turned on its head O

RADAMES & AMNERIS:

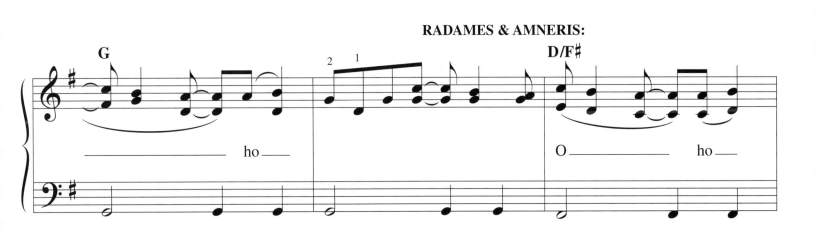

ho O ho

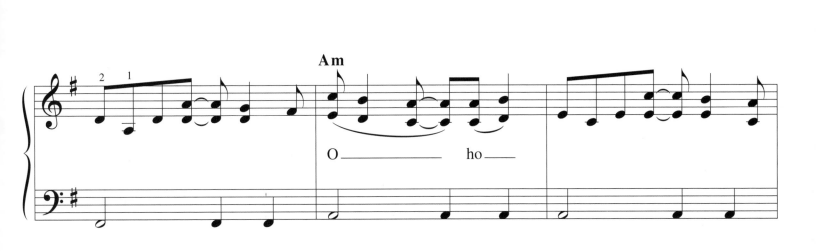

O ho

98

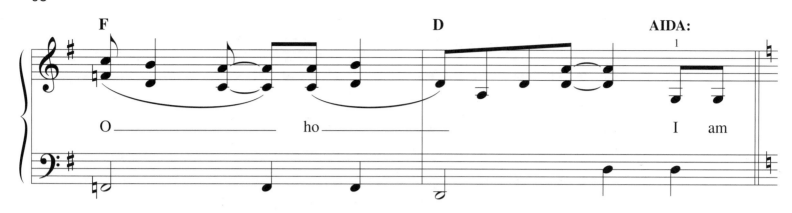

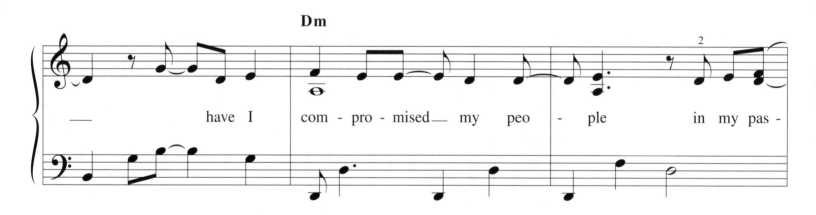

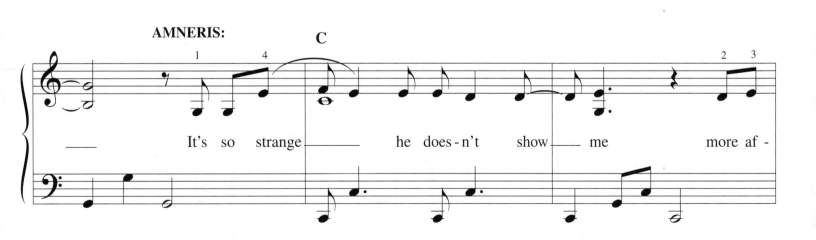

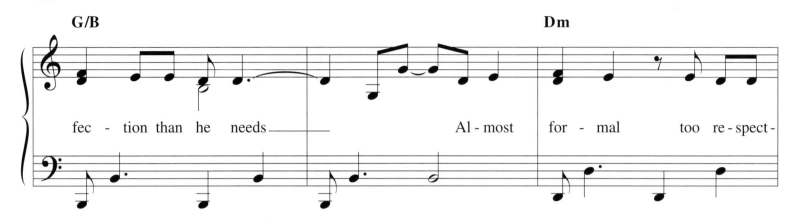

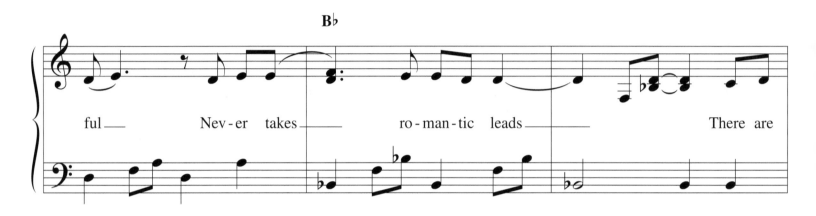

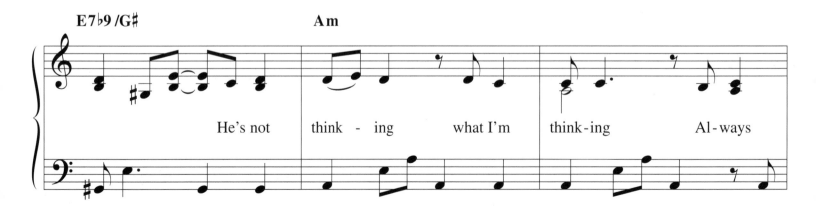

half__ a step be-hind_____ Al-ways half__ a step__ be-hind__

AIDA & RADAMES: **AIDA, AMNERIS & RADAMES:**

O_____ ho_____ O_____ ho____

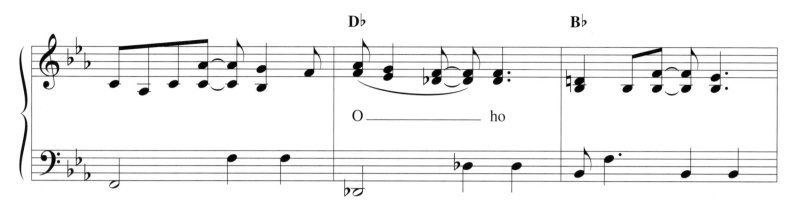

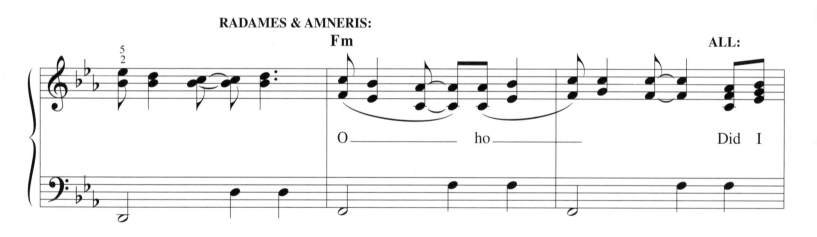

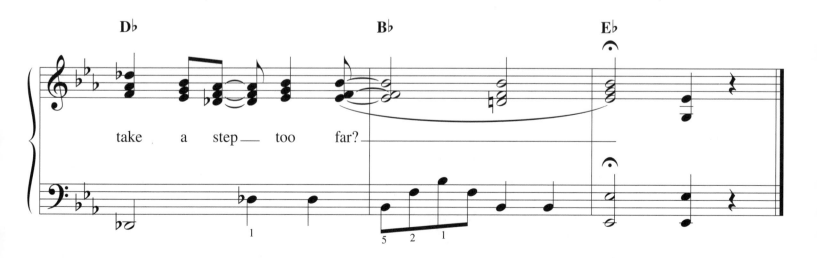

EASY AS LIFE

Music by ELTON JOHN
Lyrics by TIM RICE

All I have to do   is for - get how much I

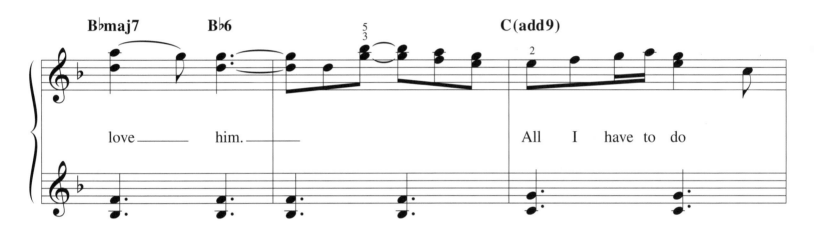

love_____ him._____   All   I   have to do

is put my long - ing to one side.

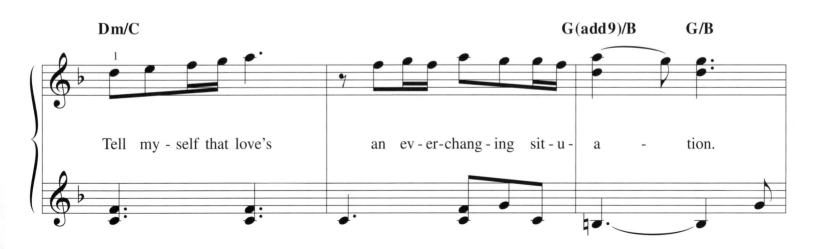

Tell my - self that love's   an ev - er - chang - ing sit - u - a - tion.

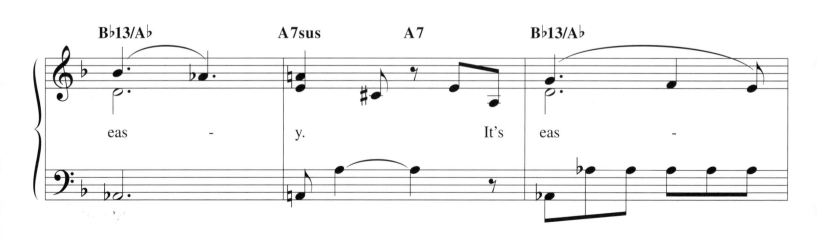

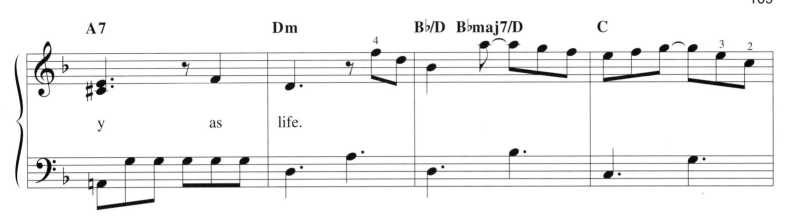

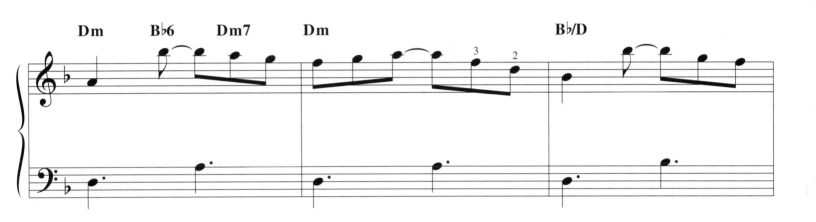

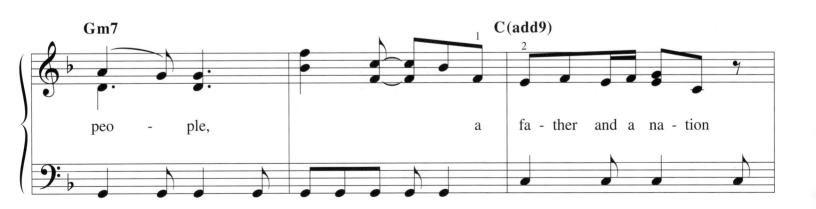

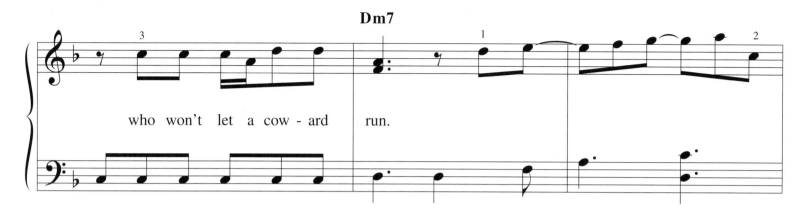

who won't let a cow - ard run.

Is this how the gods re-ward the faith-ful through the ag - es?

Forc-ing us to prove that all the hard-est things we've

done are eas -

y, so— eas-y. And

though I'll think a-bout him till the earth draws in a- round— me,

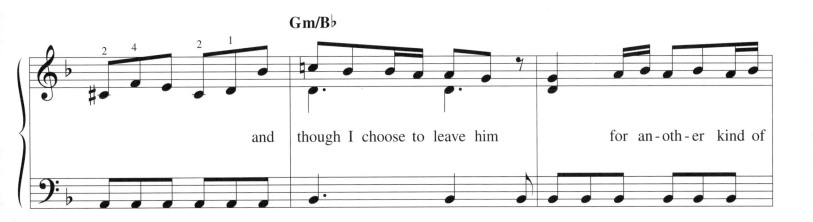

and though I choose to leave him for an-oth-er kind of

love, this is no de-ni- al,

112

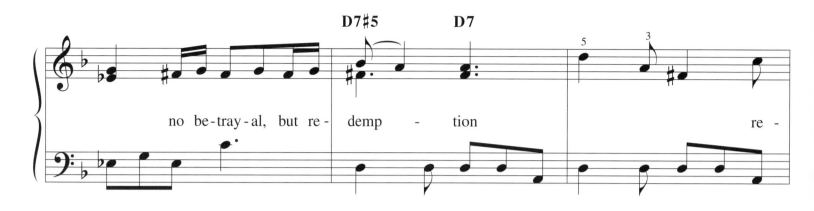

no be-tray-al, but re- demp - tion re -

deemed in my own eyes and in the pan-the-on a - bove.

It's eas - y. It's

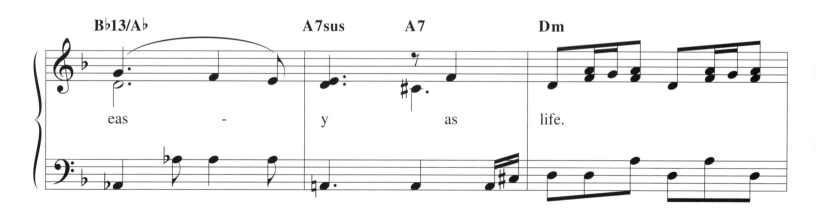

eas - y as life.

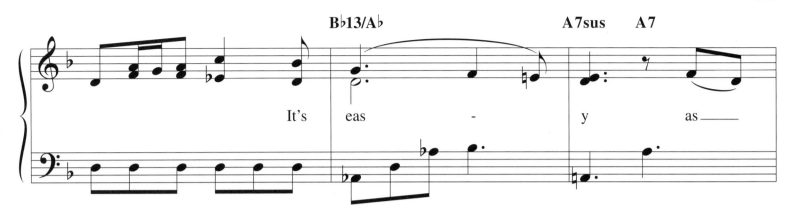

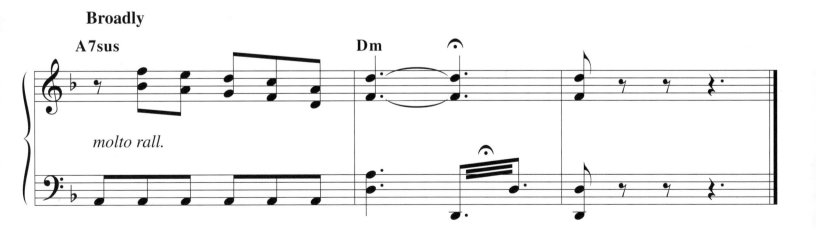

LIKE FATHER, LIKE SON

Music by ELTON JOHN
Lyrics by TIM RICE

D 7/F♯

C/G

do - ing just what I'd have done._____ Like Fa - ther

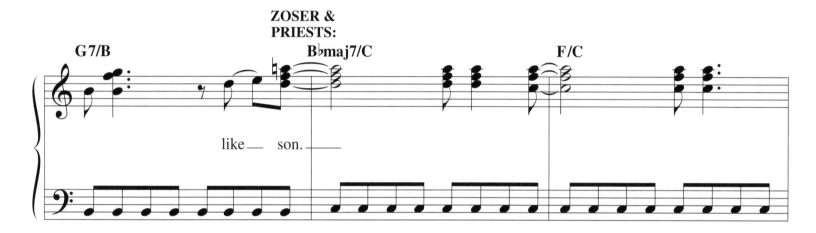

**ZOSER &
PRIESTS:**

G 7/B

B♭maj7/C

F/C

like__ son._____

C

F

C

RADAMES:

Don't as - sume____ your vic - es get____ hand - ed down__

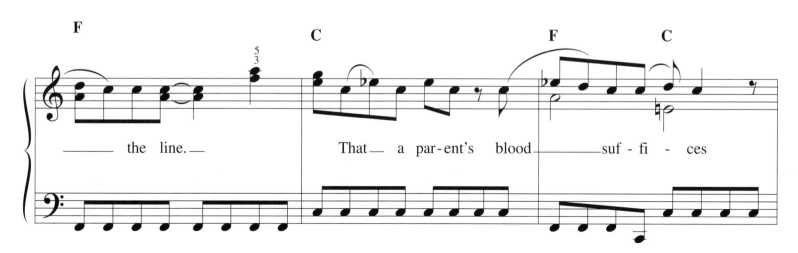

F

C

F

C

____ the line.____ That__ a par - ent's blood_____ suf - fi - ces

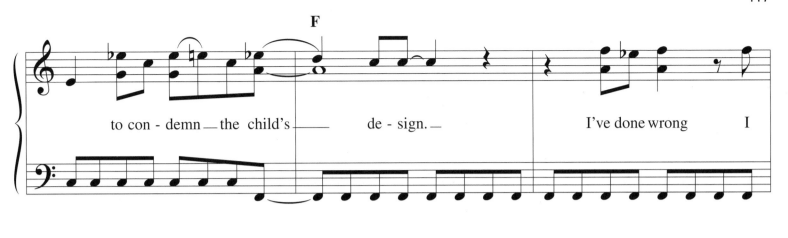

to con - demn the child's de - sign. I've done wrong I

can't de - ny but at least I know that I

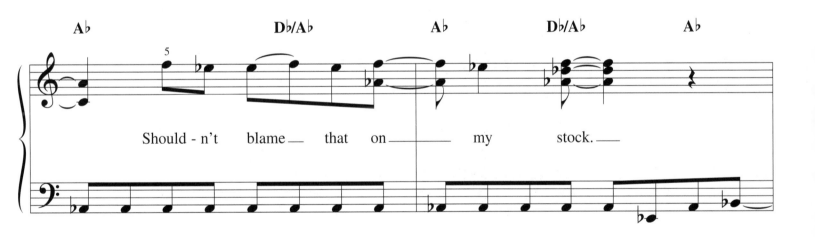

Should - n't blame that on my stock.

This may come as quite a shock but I'm no chip off an -

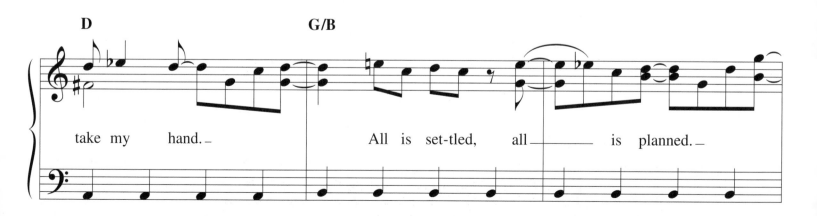

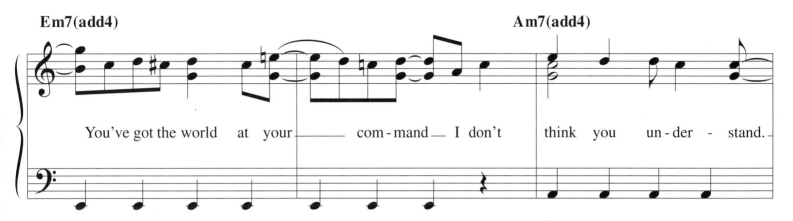

Em7(add4)   Am7(add4)

You've got the world at your com-mand I don't think you un-der - stand.

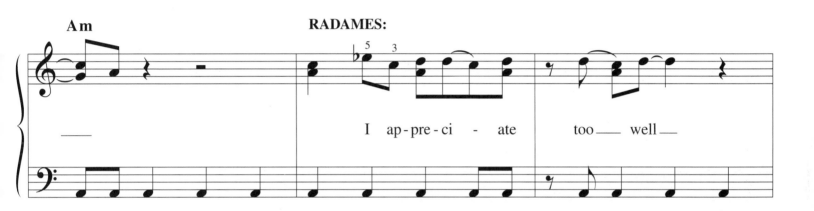

Am   RADAMES:

I ap-pre-ci - ate too — well —

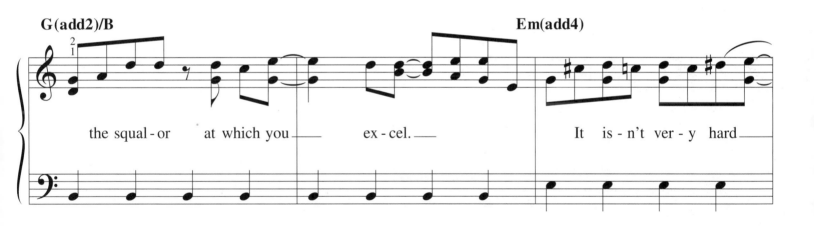

G(add2)/B   Em(add4)

the squal - or at which you — ex - cel. — It is - n't ver - y hard —

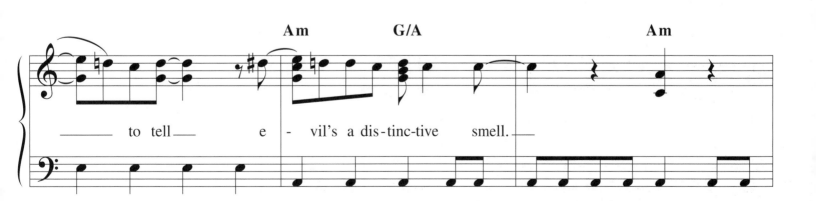

Am   G/A   Am

— to tell — e - vil's a dis-tinc-tive smell. —

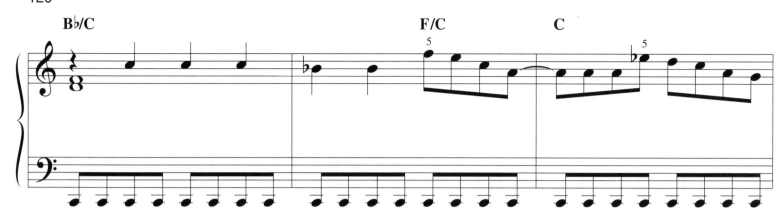

He's — lost all sense — of rea - son

And — why? — Some — for-eign slut. — Not — on - ly is —

— that trea - son Some — doors — are slam - ming shut.

ZOSER & PRIESTS:

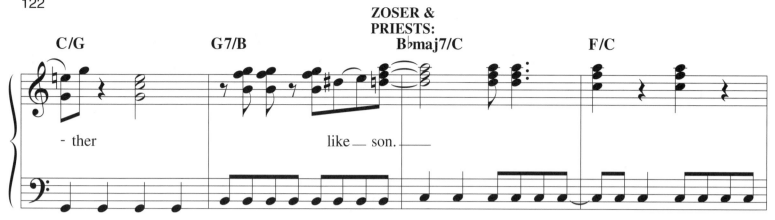

-ther   like — son.

Like Fa - ther   like   son.—

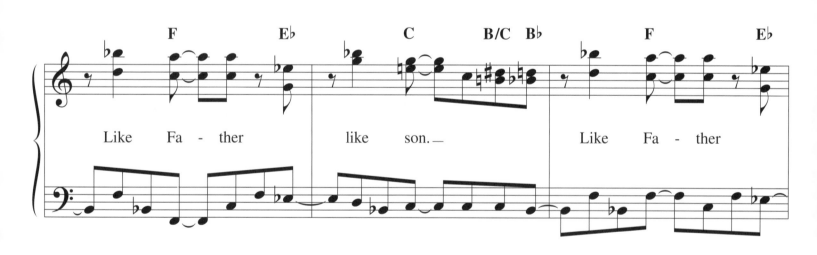

Like Fa - ther   like   son.—   Like   Fa - ther

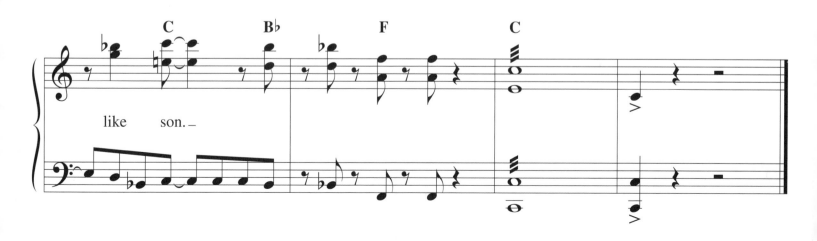

like   son.—

RADAMES' LETTER

Music by ELTON JOHN
Lyrics by TIM RICE

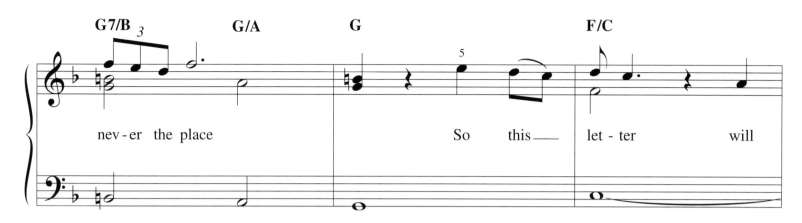

nev-er the place So this —— let - ter will

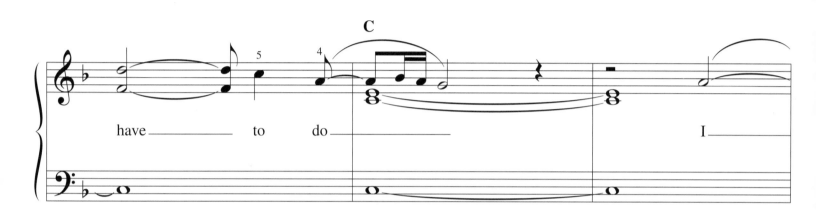

have —————— to do —————————— I ————

love ————————— you.

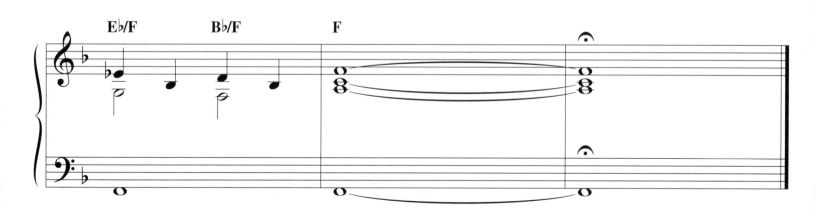

WRITTEN IN THE STARS

Music by ELTON JOHN
Lyrics by TIM RICE

(Male:) Here I am to tell___ you we can nev - er meet a - gain.

Sim - ple real - ly,___ is - n't it?___ A word or two and then a

life - time of not know - ing where or how or why or when. You

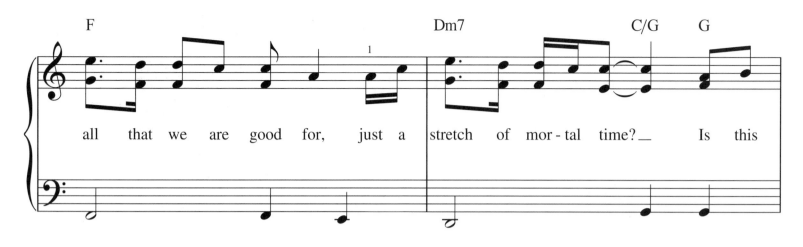

all that we are good for, just a stretch of mor-tal time?__ Is this

God's ex-per-i-ment__ in which we have no say?__ In which we're giv-en par-a-dise, but

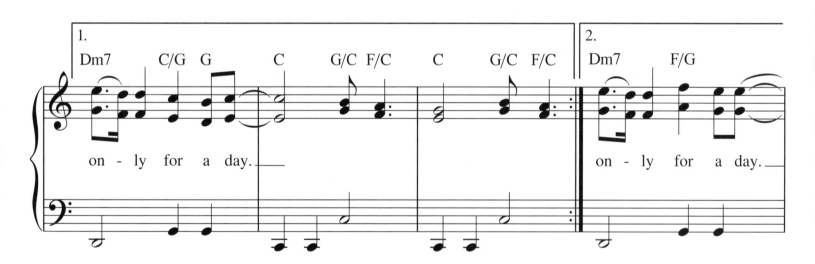

on-ly for a day.__

on-ly for a day.__

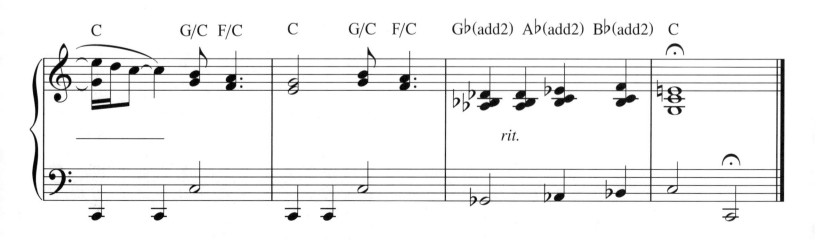

I KNOW THE TRUTH

Music by ELTON JOHN
Lyrics by TIM RICE

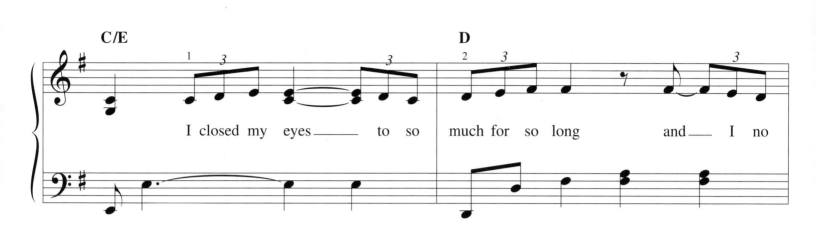

I closed my eyes _____ to so much for so long _____ and _ I no

long - er _ can _ I try to blame it on _ for - tune

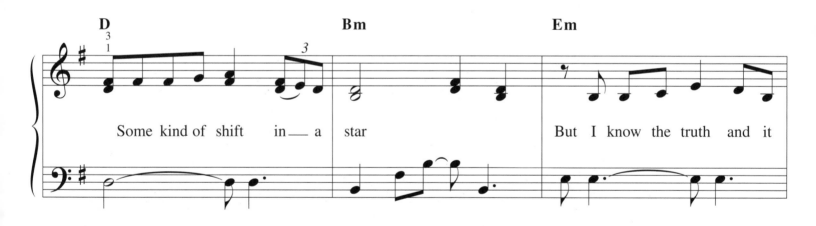

Some kind of shift in _ a star But I know the truth and it

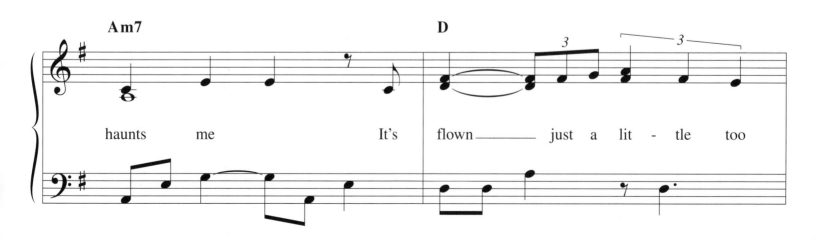

haunts me It's flown _____ just a lit - tle too

133

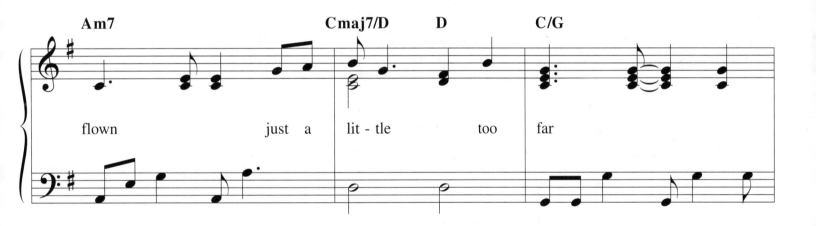

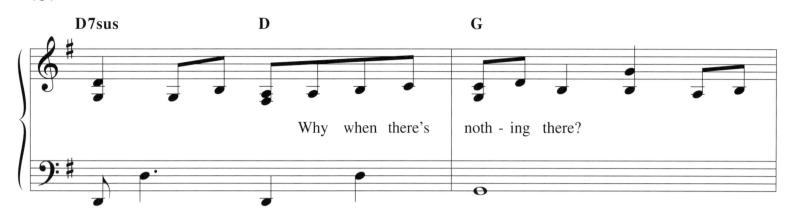

Why when there's noth - ing there?

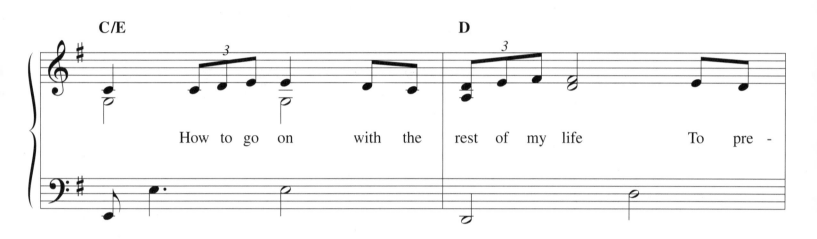

How to go on with the rest of my life To pre -

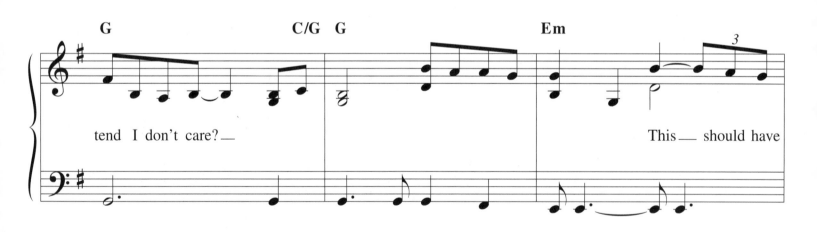

tend I don't care? — This — should have

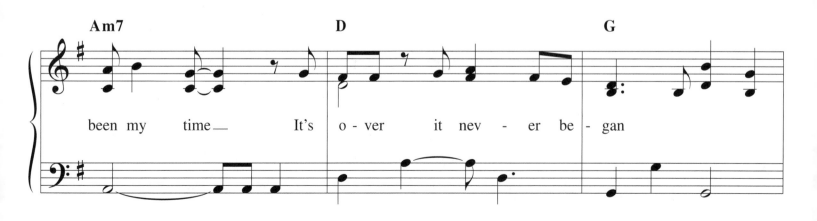

been my time — It's o - ver it nev - er be - gan

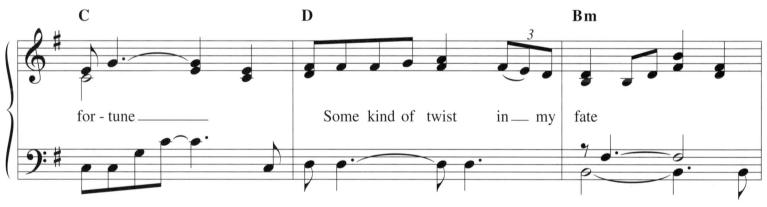

late

I know the truth— and it mocks me —

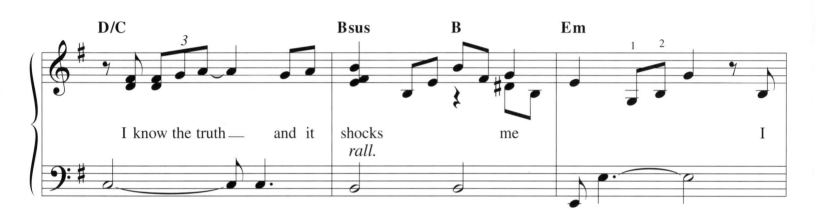

I know the truth— and it shocks me

rall.

I

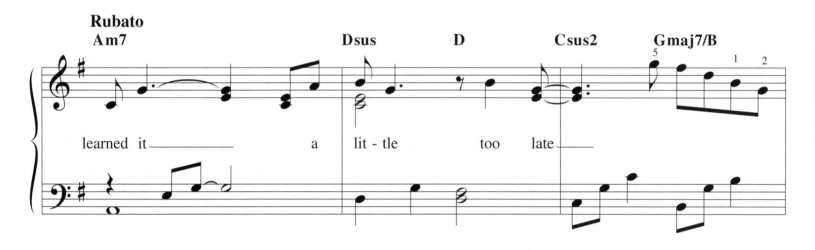

Rubato

learned it———— a lit-tle too late———

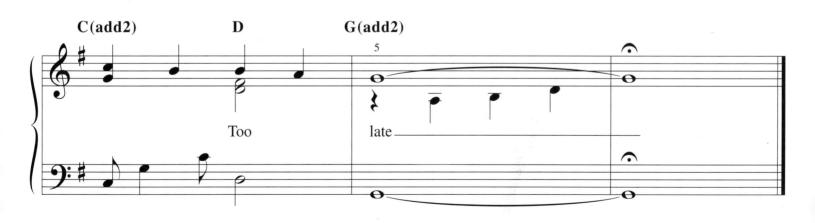

Too late —